CHILD HEALTH CARE SUPPORT PROGRAMS FOR DEAFNESS, DENTAL SERVICES AND DOWN SYNDROME

CHILDREN'S ISSUES, LAWS AND PROGRAMS

Additional books in this series can be found on Nova's website under the Series tab.

Additional E-books in this series can be found on Nova's website under the E-books tab.

HEALTH CARE ISSUES, COSTS AND ACCESS

Additional books in this series can be found on Nova's website under the Series tab.

Additional E-books in this series can be found on Nova's website under the E-books tab.

CHILD HEALTH CARE SUPPORT PROGRAMS FOR DEAFNESS, DENTAL SERVICES AND DOWN SYNDROME

Weidong Yang
and
Xiaoying Wen
EDITORS

Nova Science Publishers, Inc.
New York

For permission to use material from this book please contact us:
Telephone 631-231-7269; Fax 631-231-8175
Web Site: http://www.novapublishers.com

NOTICE TO THE READER

The Publisher has taken reasonable care in the preparation of this book, but makes no expressed or implied warranty of any kind and assumes no responsibility for any errors or omissions. No liability is assumed for incidental or consequential damages in connection with or arising out of information contained in this book. The Publisher shall not be liable for any special, consequential, or exemplary damages resulting, in whole or in part, from the readers' use of, or reliance upon, this material. Any parts of this book based on government reports are so indicated and copyright is claimed for those parts to the extent applicable to compilations of such works.

Independent verification should be sought for any data, advice or recommendations contained in this book. In addition, no responsibility is assumed by the publisher for any injury and/or damage to persons or property arising from any methods, products, instructions, ideas or otherwise contained in this publication.

This publication is designed to provide accurate and authoritative information with regard to the subject matter covered herein. It is sold with the clear understanding that the Publisher is not engaged in rendering legal or any other professional services. If legal or any other expert assistance is required, the services of a competent person should be sought. FROM A DECLARATION OF PARTICIPANTS JOINTLY ADOPTED BY A COMMITTEE OF THE AMERICAN BAR ASSOCIATION AND A COMMITTEE OF PUBLISHERS.

Additional color graphics may be available in the e-book version of this book.

Library of Congress Cataloging-in-Publication Data

Child health care support programs for deafness, dental services and Down syndrome / editors, Weidong Yang and Xiaoying Wen.
    p. cm.
  Includes bibliographical references and index.
  ISBN 978-1-61470-970-1 (hardcover)
  1. Deaf children--United States--Language. 2. Children--Dental care--United States. 3. Down syndrome--United States. 4. Child health services--United States. I. Yang, Weidong. II. Wen, Xiaoying.
  HV2551.C35 2011
  362.1083'0973--dc23
                                                                                              2011028040

Published by Nova Science Publishers, Inc. ✛ *New York*

CONTENTS

PREFACE

This book explores federal health care support programs that have been instituted to treat children that are deaf and hard of hearing and to improve children's dental services and oral health care, as well as medical care programs for children with Down Syndrome and their special health care concerns. The federal government supports these children through the Early Hearing Detection and Intervention (EHDI) program, which awards grants to states to develop systems to screen and diagnose newborns and infants for hearing loss. The Children's Health Insurance Program Reauthorization Act of 2009 studies children's access to dental care; and the Prenatally and Postnally Diagnosed Conditions Awareness Act focuses on the effectiveness of current health care and family support programs for the families of children with disabilities.

Chapter 1- Deaf and hard of hearing children can face significant challenges developing the language and literacy skills needed to succeed in school and become self-sufficient adults. The federal government supports these children through the Early Hearing Detection and Intervention (EHDI) program, which awards grants to states to develop systems to screen and diagnose newborns and infants for hearing loss and refer them for appropriate interventions. Also, the Individuals with Disabilities Education Act (IDEA) supports and funds early intervention and special education services for children with disabilities, including deafness and hearing loss.

Chapter 2- The Children's Health Insurance Program Reauthorization Act of 2009 (CHIPRA) required GAO to study children's access to dental care. GAO assessed (1) the extent to which dentists participate in Medicaid and the Children's Health Insurance Program (CHIP) and federal efforts to help families find participating dentists; (2) data on access for Medicaid and CHIP children in different states and in managed care; (3) federal efforts to improve access in underserved areas; and (4) how states and other countries have used mid-level dental providers to improve children's access. To do this, GAO (1) examined state reported dentist participation and the Department of Health and Human Services's (HHS) Insure Kids Now Web site for all 50 states and the District of Columbia and called a non-representative sample of dentists in four states; (2) reviewed national data on provision of Medicaid dental services and use of managed care; (3) interviewed HHS officials and assessed certain HHS dental programs; and (4) interviewed officials in eight states and four countries on the use of mid-level and other dental providers.

Chapter 3- On October 8, 2008, the Prenatally and Postnatally Diagnosed Conditions Awareness Act was signed into law, requiring GAO to submit a report concerning the effectiveness of current health care and family support programs for the families of children with disabilities. In this report, GAO focused on Down syndrome because it is a medical condition that is associated with disabilities and occurs frequently enough to yield a sufficient population size for an analysis.

In: Child Health Care Support Programs ...   ISBN: 978-1-61470-970-1
Editors: W. Y. and X. Wen   © 2012 Nova Science Publishers, Inc.

Chapter 1

DEAF AND HARD OF HEARING CHILDREN: FEDERAL SUPPORT FOR DEVELOPING LANGUAGE AND LITERACY[*]

United States Government Accountability Office

WHY GAO DID THIS STUDY

Deaf and hard of hearing children can face significant challenges developing the language and literacy skills needed to succeed in school and become self-sufficient adults. The federal government supports these children through the Early Hearing Detection and Intervention (EHDI) program, which awards grants to states to develop systems to screen and diagnose newborns and infants for hearing loss and refer them for appropriate interventions. Also, the Individuals with Disabilities Education Act (IDEA) supports and funds early intervention and special education services for children with disabilities, including deafness and hearing loss.

To better understand how federal programs support deaf and hard of hearing children, GAO was asked to examine the: (1) extent of hearing loss

---

[*] This is an edited, reformatted and augmented version of the United States Government Accountability Office publication, Report to Congressional Requesters GAO-11-357, dated May 2011.

among children, (2) settings in which these children are educated, (3) factors that help deaf and hard of hearing children acquire language and literacy skills, and (4) challenges to providing appropriate interventions for these children. GAO analyzed data on hearing loss; reviewed research literature; interviewed educators, national organizations, parents, and state and federal officials; and examined relevant federal laws and regulations. A draft of this report was provided to the Departments of Education and Health and Human Services for review and comment. Each provided technical comments, which were incorporated into the report, as appropriate. GAO makes no recommendations in this report.

WHAT GAO FOUND

Available data indicate hearing loss affects a small percentage of children. In 2008, the prevalence of hearing loss among infants under 12 months was 0.1 percent, or about 1 diagnosed case per 1,000 screened. While the Centers for Disease Control and Prevention (CDC) does not collect hearing test data for children under age 12, other than EHDI data, federal surveys conducted from 2005 to 2009 estimated 3 percent or fewer of children nationwide under age 12 had hearing problems. Based on nationwide hearing examination data for youth aged 12–17 from 2005 to 2008, an estimated 1 percent had at least moderate hearing loss in one or both ears.

Deaf and hard of hearing children are educated in a variety of settings, from regular classrooms to separate schools for the deaf. Data from the U.S. Department of Education (Education) indicate that in fall 2008 the majority of these children who received special education did so in regular early childhood programs or regular classrooms for at least part of their day.

Experts GAO interviewed agreed that several key factors are critical for helping deaf and hard of hearing children acquire language and literacy skills. Early exposure to language—either spoken or signed—is critical because during the first few years of life it is easiest for children to learn language. Also, parents need to have information on the full range of communication options available so that they can make informed choices to meet their children's individual needs. Similarly, experts told GAO that education for these children should be individualized and that there should not be one standard approach for educating them. Additionally, having skilled professionals, such as qualified interpreters in regular classrooms, is important for ensuring that children with hearing loss receive the same information as their hearing classmates.

Limited information and resources are challenges to providing deaf and hard of hearing children with appropriate interventions. Experts indicated that parents may not always receive information on the full range of communication options available, and may not understand the importance of enrolling their children in early intervention services. Additionally, a lack of data can limit efforts to evaluate early intervention outcomes. The EHDI law calls for CDC and the Health Resources and Services Administration in the Department of Health and Human Services (HHS) to support states in the evaluation of early intervention efforts—programs that are, in part, provided under IDEA. These agencies suggested that privacy requirements may restrict the information that EHDI and early intervention programs can share, limiting efforts to evaluate outcomes for children. However, HHS and Education are taking a number of steps to identify best practices for sharing data and tracking the outcomes of deaf and hard of hearing children who receive early intervention services. Experts also cited a shortage of qualified teachers and interpreters as a major challenge. Moreover, providing services for these students can be costly and it is difficult for schools to provide a variety of options, especially in rural areas.

ABBREVIATIONS

CDC	Centers for Disease Control and Prevention
Education	U.S. Department of Education
EHDI	Early Hearing Detection and Intervention
HHS	U.S. Department of Health and Human Services
HRSA	Health Resources and Services Administration
IDEA	Individuals with Disabilities Education Act

May 25, 2011
The Honorable Tom Harkin, Chairman
Committee on Health, Education, Labor, and Pensions
United States Senate

The Honorable George Miller, Ranking Member
Committee on Education and the Workforce
House of Representatives

Children who are deaf or hard of hearing[1] can face considerable challenges developing the language and literacy skills they need to succeed in school and become self-sufficient, productive adults. Although experts suggest that deaf and hard of hearing children who receive appropriate educational and other services can successfully transition to adulthood, research indicates that many do not receive the necessary support early on or during their school years to keep up with their hearing peers. For example, according to one study, the median reading comprehension score of deaf or hard of hearing students at age 18 was below the median of fourth-grade hearing students.[2]

In response to your interest in how federal programs support deaf and hard of hearing children, this report provides information on: (1) the extent of hearing loss among children in the United States, (2) the settings in which these children are educated, (3) factors that have been shown to help deaf and hard of hearing children acquire language and literacy skills, and (4) challenges that exist to providing appropriate interventions for these children.

To respond to the first objective, we analyzed available data from hearing tests and several national surveys conducted from 2005 to 2009. We assessed the reliability of the survey data by (1) performing electronic testing of required data elements, (2) reviewing existing information about the data and the system that produced them, and (3) interviewing agency officials knowledgeable about the data. We determined that the data were sufficiently reliable for the purposes of this report. To address the second objective, we analyzed 2008 special education data—the most recent data available—on the Individuals with Disabilities Education Act reported to the U.S. Department of Education (Education). For our third objective, we interviewed experts from national organizations representing educators, parents, and the deaf community to obtain their views on the acquisition of language and literacy skills in deaf and hard of hearing children. We also reviewed published literature from 2005 to 2010 to identify factors associated with deaf and hard of hearing students' language and literacy development. To address our fourth objective, we reviewed federal supports for children with hearing loss—such as the Early Hearing Detection and Intervention program and programs under the Individuals with Disabilities Education Act that serve children with disabilities—and relevant federal laws, regulations, and guidance. We interviewed officials from Education and the U.S. Department of Health and Human Services (HHS) responsible for administering these programs and experts from national organizations. We also conducted site visits to Colorado, Massachusetts, and Washington—states which varied in the percentage of children with hearing loss educated in regular classrooms and in the characteristics of their state schools for the deaf. During the visits we spoke with state, school district, and school officials about state and local efforts to provide educational services to deaf and hard of hearing children, as well as any challenges and gaps in services for these students. We also interviewed parents of deaf and hard of hearing children about their views on their children's educational experiences. See appendix I for additional information on our scope and methodology.

We conducted this performance audit from March 2010 to May 2011 in accordance with generally accepted government auditing standards. Those standards require that we plan and perform the audit to obtain sufficient, appropriate evidence to provide a reasonable basis for our findings and conclusions based on our audit objectives. We believe that the evidence obtained provides a reasonable basis for our findings and conclusions based on our audit objectives.

BACKGROUND

Hearing Loss among Children

Hearing loss can vary by type, level of severity, age at onset, and cause. Experts generally agree on the major types of hearing loss: conductive, sensorineural, and mixed (see table 1).[3]

Hearing loss can also be classified by its level of severity and whether one or both ears are affected. The level of loss can range from slight to profound.[4] Hearing loss may be present in one ear (unilateral) or in both ears (bilateral). The level of loss in the two ears may be the same or different.

Hearing loss may be present at birth or may develop later. It can also be described as sudden or progressive (worsening over time), and stable or fluctuating. The National Institute on Deafness and Other Communication Disorders reports that about 50–60 percent of severe to profound cases of childhood hearing loss are due to genetic causes.[5] However, about 90 percent of infants who are born deaf are born to hearing parents. Experts also suggest nearly 25 percent of children with hearing loss have one or more other developmental disability, such as cerebral palsy or vision loss.

Table 1. Types of Hearing Loss

Type of hearing loss	Description
Conductive	Conductive hearing loss results when sounds are prevented fromgoing through the outer or middle ear, such as by a malformation of part of the ear or ear infections. This type of hearing loss can often be corrected with medicine or surgery.
Sensorineural	Sensorineural hearing loss occurs when there is a problem in theway the inner ear or hearing nerve works, such as from illness or noise exposure.
Mixed	Mixed hearing loss includes both conductive and sensorineural hearing loss.

Sources: Centers for Disease Control and Prevention and the American Speech-Language-Hearing Association.

There are two primary types of personal assistive devices used to improve children's hearing—hearing aids and cochlear implants.[6] Hearing aids amplify sound and can be worn by children as young as infants.[7] According to the Centers for Disease Control and Prevention, children with severe to profound hearing loss may benefit from a cochlear implant. Unlike hearing aids, cochlear implants are surgically implanted devices that process sound from the environment and ultimately signal the brain, which can learn to recognize these signals in a meaningful way. According to available data from the U.S. Food and Drug Administration, as of April 2009, about 25,500 children in the United States had received cochlear implants.

Communication Modes for Deaf and Hard of Hearing Children

Deaf and hard of hearing children can communicate in a variety of ways, including signing and speaking. Signing can take many forms, including American Sign Language, which is a complete and complex language with its own syntax and grammar that uses a combination of signs made with the hands and other movements, such as facial expressions and postures of the body. Other forms of visual communication are based on spoken language, such as Cued Speech—which uses hand shapes to represent different sounds in the English language, for example—and can aid lipreading.

Signing Exact English is a sign system that corresponds to literal English. A communication mode may also combine the use of signing with speech. A survey of deaf and hard of hearing students in 2007–2008 found that more than half, nationwide, learned in speech-only environments (see figure 1).

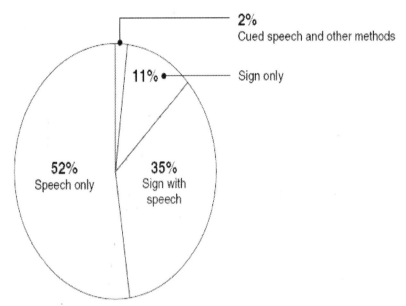

Source: Gallaudet Research Institute (November 2008). Regional and National Summary Report of Data from the 2007-08 Annual Survey of Deaf and Hard of Hearing Children and Youth. Washington, DC: GRI, Gallaudet University.

Figure 1. Percentage of Deaf and Hard of Hearing Students by Primary Communication Mode Used for Instruction.

Federal Support for Children with Hearing Loss

From birth through age 21, the federal government supports the educational needs of deaf and hard of hearing children, and other children with disabilities, through a variety of means (see figure 2).

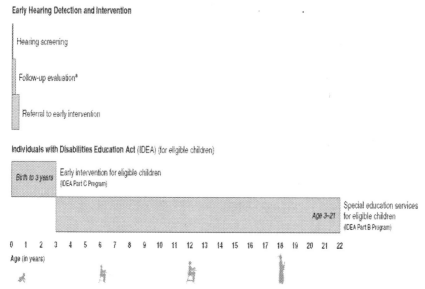

Source: GAO analysis of select federal laws and programs.

[a] For infants who screen positive for hearing loss.

Figure 2. Federal Support for Children with Hearing Loss.

Early Hearing Detection and Intervention (EHDI)

HHS, through its Centers for Disease Control and Prevention (CDC) and Health Resources and Services Administration (HRSA), provides grants and assistance to states to develop, monitor, and collect data on early hearing screening, evaluation, and intervention programs and systems.[8] The Joint Committee on Infant Hearing[9] developed national program goals for early screening and intervention that aim to ensure that all newborns are screened for hearing loss before 1 month of age, that infants who do not pass the screening receive a full evaluation before 3 months, and that those identified with hearing loss receive early intervention services before 6 months.[10] Congress reauthorized the EHDI program in December 2010, with amendments specifying that the purpose of the grants is to help states develop programs to ensure that children who are referred from state screening programs receive prompt evaluation and diagnosis and the appropriate educational, audiological, and medical interventions.[11]

Individuals with Disabilities Education Act (IDEA)

To support the educational needs of children with disabilities, including those who are deaf or hard of hearing, Congress originally enacted IDEA in

1975,[12] most recently reauthorizing and amending it in 2004.[13] IDEA authorizes federal funding for early intervention and special education and related services for children with disabilities through two main programs: the Infants and Toddlers with Disabilities (Part C) program,[14] which supports early intervention services for children younger than 3 years of age, and the Assistance for Education of All Children with Disabilities (Part B) program,[15] which supports the special education needs of children aged 3– 21 (see appendix II).[16] While IDEA Part C and B programs have different eligibility criteria and children are evaluated for each program separately, Education considers the effective transition between the programs a priority and requires states to support families through a timely transition process.[17] States are also required by IDEA to develop transition plans for children exiting the Part C program.

As a condition of receiving IDEA funds, states must meet several requirements, including:

- identifying and evaluating all children with disabilities to determine whether they are eligible for early intervention or special education and related services;
- providing early intervention in accordance with an individualized family service plan[18] (Part C) or special education and services in accordance with an individualized education program[19] (Part B), as developed by a team that includes the parent and qualified professionals; and,
- to the maximum extent appropriate, providing early intervention services in a natural environment and educating children with disabilities with children who are not disabled.[20]

As of fall 2008, more than 78,000 deaf and hard of hearing children aged 3– 21 in the 50 states received services under IDEA Part B,[21] or about 1 percent of all students served by IDEA Part B nationwide (see figure 3).

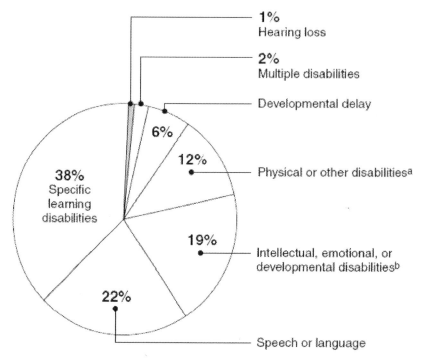

Source: U.S. Department of Education data from www.ideadata.org.

Note: This figure likely represents an undercount of all children 3–21 with hearing loss served under IDEA, as data are collected by primary disability. According to Education, data for children up to age 3 are not available by disability category under the Part C program.

[a] Physical or other disabilities category includes orthopedic impairments, visual impairments, deaf-blindness, traumatic brain injury, and other health impairments.

[b] Intellectual, emotional, or developmental disabilities category includes intellectual disabilities, emotional disturbance, and autism.

Figure 3. Percentage of All Students Aged 3–21 in the 50 States Served by IDEA in 2008 by Primary Disability.

HEARING LOSS AFFECTS A SMALL PERCENTAGE OF CHILDREN

According to the most recent hearing screening data available from CDC's EHDI program, the prevalence of hearing loss among newborns and infants younger than 12 months in 2008 was approximately 0.1 percent, or about 1 diagnosed case for every 1,000 screened.[22] That year, more than 3 million infants, or 97 percent of births nationwide, were screened for hearing loss. Of those screened, 2 percent failed.[23] Further audiological testing for those infants who failed a screening revealed that about 7 percent were subsequently diagnosed with hearing loss and about 41 percent were diagnosed with normal hearing. However, further information on the hearing status for the majority (53 percent) of these children was unavailable to CDC for a variety of reasons; most often, states reported that families could not be contacted or were unresponsive.[24] As a result there is no information available to CDC to confirm hearing loss in more than half of infants who failed their hearing screening test that year. It should be noted that the recent reauthorization of the EHDI program included a provision that may help remedy this problem. Specifically, the reauthorization amended the EHDI law to provide that funding to states can be used to develop efficient models to ensure that those who fail an initial screening receive follow-up care by a qualified health care provider and that states will be encouraged to adopt models to increase the rate of follow-up for these children.[25]

Data on children beyond infancy similarly suggest a low prevalence of hearing loss. While the CDC does not currently collect hearing test data for children younger than the age of 12, apart from the data collected under the EHDI program,[26] HHS surveys from 2005 to 2009 indicate an estimated 3 percent or fewer of children nationwide in this age range had hearing problems.[27] (See appendix III for more information.) In addition to the EHDI program, the CDC sponsors hearing examinations of youth from ages 12 through 19 through the National Health and Nutrition Examination Survey.[28] Based on these examinations from 2005 to 2008, an estimated 1 percent of 12–17 year olds nationwide had at least moderate hearing loss in one or both ears.[29] When we compared the demographic characteristics of those with moderate to moderately-severe hearing loss to those with normal hearing to mild loss, we found no statistically significant differences in the distributions of sex, race, or poverty status[30] between the two groups.

MOST DEAF AND HARD OF HEARING CHILDREN ARE EDUCATED IN REGULAR CLASSROOMS

Children who are deaf or hard of hearing are educated in a variety of settings, ranging from regular classrooms alongside hearing peers to separate schools and residential facilities for children with hearing loss. According to data from Education, the majority of deaf and hard of hearing children who received special education through IDEA Part B in fall 2008 did so in regular early childhood programs or regular classrooms, for at least part of their day (see table 2).

Table 2. Educational Settings of Children with Hearing Loss in the 50 States Served Under IDEA Part B in Fall 2008

Educational setting for children ages 3–5	Percentage of children ages 3–5	Educational setting for children ages 6–21	Percentage of children ages 6–21
In regular early childhood program more than 80% of time	32.9%	In regular classroom more than 80% of time	53.3%
In regular early childhood program 40–79% of time	6.7	In regular classroom 40–79% of time	17.2
In regular early childhood program less than 40% of time	13	In regular classroom less than 40% of time	15.8
Separate classroom[a]	26.6	n/a	n/a
Separate school	13.5	Separate school	8.2
Other[b]	4	Other[b]	4.7
Data unavailable[c]	3.4	Data unavailable[c]	0.9

Source: GAO analysis of Education data from www.ideadata.org.

Note: Data in each column do not sum to 100 due to rounding.

[a] Separate classroom is not an available category for students aged 6 to 21.

[b] Other may include placement in a private school by parents or residential or correctional facilities, home or hospital environments, or service provider locations.

[c] Data that are unavailable were either not reported to Education or suppressed to limit disclosure due to the small number of children.

Under IDEA, the degree of a child's hearing loss alone should not dictate a particular educational setting. According to the law, decisions about the setting in which deaf or hard of hearing children are educated should be based on consideration of a child's language and communication needs, oppor-tunities for direct communication with peers, and access to instruction in the language and communication mode the child uses, among other factors. During our site visits, we observed deaf and hard of hearing students in regular classrooms with hearing students, aided by interpreters; in self-contained classrooms of deaf and hard of hearing children in local public schools; and in schools for the deaf. Students may also divide their time among multiple educational settings. We also observed students who spent most of their time in a self-contained classroom but attended some classes, such as art and music, with hearing peers, and met with students who divided their time between a deaf school and a regular classroom in a local public school. Students from deaf schools may choose to participate in other public school programs in order to take advantage of advanced placement courses or other course offerings not available in the deaf school.

EARLY EXPOSURE TO LANGUAGE AND AN INDIVIDUALLY TAILORED EDUCATION ARE VITAL TO DEVELOPING LANGUAGE AND LITERACY SKILLS

Early Access to Language Helps Deaf and Hard of Hearing Children Build Language and Literacy Skills

Experts we spoke with stated that it is important to expose deaf and hard of hearing children to language as early as possible in life. They told us that the first few years of a child's life are the most critical for learning language because it is during this time when the brain is rapidly developing that it is easiest to learn language. Several educators we spoke with shared stories of deaf children who did not receive services until later in childhood and subsequently lagged behind. Officials at one school also said that the age at which children are first exposed to language is a good predictor of their future language skills. Research into language development bears this out. One study examining children with moderate to profound hearing loss compared those who were exposed to language through an early intervention program before they were 3 months of age with those who enrolled later. The study found that by the time these children were 12 to 16 months old, those who started earlier were already demonstrating more advanced language skills.[31]

The benefits of early language exposure are not tied to any one language or communication mode. Experts we interviewed agreed that early exposure aids deaf and hard of hearing children in the acquisition of language skills, whether the language is signed or spoken. A study focusing on children with cochlear implants found that those who received an implant before 2 1/2 years of age developed speech more rapidly and had better pronunciation and vocabulary than children who received an implant at an older age.[32] Similarly, research indicates that children exposed to sign language early and consistently develop larger vocabularies more quickly than those who are not.[33]

Experts and advocates we interviewed also indicated that it is important for parents to have access to information on the full range of communication options. They told us that informed parents are better able to make decisions about communication modes and assistive technologies that meet the needs of their children. In laying out principles for EHDI programs, the Joint Committee on Infant Hearing[34] in 2007 stated that families should be made aware of all communication modes and available assistive hearing technologies. The committee added that a family's decision-making process should be guided by informed choices and desired outcomes. Because children can benefit from early intervention regardless of their communication mode, knowing the range of options can help a family make a decision that best suits its needs.

Education Should Be Individualized, Including Delivery by Qualified Professionals with Knowledge of Hearing-Related Issues

Educators and advocates we spoke with told us that deaf and hard of hearing children should have an education tailored to their individual abilities and needs. These experts told us that because the needs of deaf and hard of hearing children can vary widely, there should not be one standard approach for educating them. The provision of an individualized education for all children with disabilities based on their unique needs is a key requirement of IDEA. In addition, Education has issued guidance[35] to help ensure that the unique communication and related services needs of deaf and hard of children are addressed. We observed examples of schools providing individualized and flexible approaches during our visits to states. In one regional program in Massachusetts, students have the opportunity to take classes in regular classrooms with other high school students, but may spend part of their time in separate classrooms for subjects where they need extra help. Also, we visited a school in Colorado where children receive additional help in writing and vocabulary every other day in a resource center.

Educators and advocates also highlighted the importance of having staff with knowledge of hearing-related issues to provide services to deaf and hard of hearing students. Guidance from the National Association of State Directors of Special Education notes that it is important that audiologists in schools have specific training to work with these students and that teachers who work with this population also be trained in deaf education.[36] Additionally, advocates noted that having skilled interpreters is especially important for deaf children in regular classrooms because they rely on these interpreters to accurately convey to them what is being taught in the classroom.

LIMITED INFORMATION AND RESOURCES ARE CHALLENGES TO PROVIDING APPROPRIATE INTERVENTIONS TO CHILDREN

Parents May Lack Information on How to Address the Specific Needs of Their Children

Experts told us that parents do not always have access to information on the full range of available communication options. Several said that the first service provider with whom parents consult after their child is identified as having hearing loss can have a significant influence on the choices parents make, especially if they do not receive balanced information on a range of options. For example, if the family is first referred to an audiologist, experts were concerned that parents would choose a cochlear implant for their child rather than continue learning about other options such as sign language.

Some experts we interviewed were also concerned that parents of deaf and hard of hearing children may struggle to understand the information needed to make language and communication decisions for their children. The majority of these children are born to hearing parents, and as such, experts commented that families often do not know how to address the specific needs of their children. For instance, several officials we spoke with noted that many parents do not understand the importance of enrolling their children in early intervention services. To illustrate, 2008 data from CDC show that about 24 percent of children with a hearing loss eligible for early intervention services did not enroll in them.[37] As noted previously, early intervention services can have a significant impact on the development of a child.

Efforts to help parents make informed decisions for their deaf and hard of hearing children vary. For example, Colorado officials said state law requires cases of infants identified with a hearing loss to be referred to a hearing resources coordinator. This coordinator may meet with the family, explain the communication and service options available to the child, and refer the child to follow-up services. Similarly, Washington state officials told us that their state uses family resource coordinators to provide families with objective information about options and help them access services. In contrast, a national group of educators told us that most states lack a centralized contact and do not track children to ensure they receive follow-up services after being identified.

In addition to state efforts, some federal requirements concerning educating parents also exist. IDEA requires each state to have a public awareness program focused on the early identification of infants and toddlers with disabilities and a central directory that includes information on early intervention services and resources in the state. Additionally, Education funds Parent Training and Information Centers across the nation to provide parents of children with disabilities—including those who are deaf and hard of hearing—with training and information on working with early intervention and special education providers to meet the needs of their children.

Agencies are Taking Steps to Address Data Limitations that Hinder Evaluation of Early Interventions

Limited data may hinder the ability of states to evaluate the effectiveness of early intervention programs for deaf and hard of hearing children. The EHDI law directs HRSA to award grants or form cooperative agreements with states to monitor, among other things, the effectiveness of early interventions for children with hearing loss. Similarly, the law calls on CDC to award grants or form cooperative agreements to provide technical assistance with data collection for EHDI programs and to study the effectiveness of early intervention programs. State EHDI programs currently collect some outcome data, such as the number of children who are eligible for and enroll in early intervention. However, because early intervention services are provided under IDEA Part C, EHDI programs generally do not have access to the information on individual children needed to evaluate these interventions. State IDEA Part C programs are required to collect some outcome data on the children they serve. For example, state Part C programs collect information on the acquisition and early use of language among infants and toddlers receiving services as well as the number of children who receive assistance to transition out of Part C early intervention into Part B special education services. According to the National Center for Hearing Assessment and Management (NCHAM), such data could help state EHDI programs evaluate early intervention outcomes, but federal privacy laws and regulations may prohibit state EHDI programs from obtaining these data from state Part C programs. For instance, NCHAM states that IDEA Part C regulations prohibit programs from sharing personal information about children with anyone who is not a participating Part C service provider without written consent from parents.[38]

Federal agencies are taking a number of steps to help state EHDI programs obtain data they need on early intervention outcomes. For example, CDC is funding a study in a limited number of states to explore the feasibility of creating data management systems that enable states to collect data on developmental outcomes for deaf and hard of hearing children. The results of this study should be published by the end of fiscal year 2011, and CDC told us that the principal investigator has applied for additional funding in order to continue work in this area. Additionally, CDC, HRSA, and Education have provided technical assistance to NCHAM in identifying a number of recommended practices for helping state EHDI and Part C programs share data in a manner that is consistent with applicable privacy restrictions. These practices include implementing memorandums of agreement between EHDI and Part C programs specifying procedures for obtaining consent from parents to allow agencies to share data about their children.

Shortages of Qualified Professionals and the Availability of Resources
May Hinder Schools from Providing Appropriate Services

Experts told us that early intervention service providers and schools have trouble attracting and retaining qualified staff. Several of them told us that schools and service providers have difficulty retaining teachers, interpreters, and other staff because these professionals can receive better pay outside of the education system. Experts also told us that there is a shortage of teachers for the deaf and that the number of training programs for these professionals is decreasing. Poorly trained interpreters can also be a barrier to student learning because not all states have proficiency requirements for interpreters. For example, officials in Colorado said the state requires educational interpreters to demonstrate competency by meeting a minimum score on a proficiency test, whereas officials in Washington state told us that they have no comparable requirement for interpreters. More generally, officials from the Registry of Interpreters for the Deaf (RID) told us that according to published research, only about 20 percent of individuals taking the Educational Interpreter Performance Assessment (EIPA)[39] meet state standards or RID's standards.

Parents, educators, and advocates agree that while decisions about a child's education should be based on his or her unique needs as required by IDEA, the cost or availability of services often determines what a child receives. Some of these stakeholders said that schools may be hesitant to provide particular special education services because the costs incurred are prohibitive. For example, a school district may have to pay tuition for a child if the child attends a program outside the school district in order to have his or her needs met. Also, educators and advocacy groups said schools may prefer to place children in a program the school already offers in order to keep down costs. However, IDEA requires schools to provide an individualized education to children and to obtain input from a team, including knowledgeable school staff and parents, when making decisions about how to meet a child's needs. Additionally, IDEA requires school districts and states to provide recourse for parents who do not agree with individualized education program decisions for their child, including the ability to seek a due process hearing.

Experts also noted that providing services in rural areas is especially challenging. Hearing loss occurs in a small percentage of children and as such, there may be few deaf children in a given area. One expert noted that in some rural areas, it is not uncommon to have only one or two deaf children per county. In these cases, children may not have access to the same level of expertise or services as children in urban areas. For example, a Washington state official said that a rural county in that state had only one special education teacher to serve children with a range of disabilities and the one available speech-language therapist did not have a background in hearing loss issues.

CONCLUDING OBSERVATIONS

The newly reauthorized EHDI law acknowledges the importance of early access to services for children with hearing loss, in part, by encouraging states to increase follow-up rates for newborns and infants who fail a hearing screening. Meeting the needs of deaf and hard of hearing children requires an approach that begins early and is tailored to each child's needs. Given the impact that early intervention can have on a child's development and future self-sufficiency, and the level of federal funding devoted to it, the evaluation of the effectiveness of early intervention is crucial. The federally funded effort to facilitate these state evaluations is an important step and may, over time, help inform the effectiveness of early interventions for deaf and hard of hearing children.

AGENCY COMMENTS

We provided a draft of this report to Education and HHS for review and comment. Both agencies provided technical comments, which we incorporated into the report, as appropriate.

We are sending copies of this report to the Secretaries of Education and HHS, relevant congressional committees, and other interested parties. In addition, the report will be available on GAO's Web site at http://www.gao.gov.

If you or your staff have any questions about the report, please contact me at (202) 512-7215 or scottg@gao.gov. Contact points for our Offices of Congressional Relations and Public Affairs may be found on the last page of this report. GAO staff that made major contributions to this report are listed in appendix IV.

George A. Scott, Director
Education, Workforce, and
Income Security Issues

APPENDIX I:
SCOPE AND METHODOLOGY

To obtain information on the extent of hearing loss among children in the United States, we analyzed recent available data on hearing loss in children from hearing tests and three Department of Health and Human Services' (HHS) surveys from 2005 to 2009. Specifically, we analyzed hearing test data from the Early Hearing Detection and Intervention program on newborns and infants up to 12 months and from the National Health and Nutrition Examination Survey's hearing examinations of 12–17 year olds. We also analyzed survey data from the National Health Interview Survey, National Health and Nutrition Examination Survey, and the National Survey of Children's Health (see table 3). We evaluated these federal surveys for methodological rigor, as well as to determine the extent to which the data could be used to offer a national perspective on children with hearing loss.

Table 3. National Surveys of Children with Hearing Loss

Survey	Purpose	Age group analyzeda	Web sites, as of April 12, 2011
National Health Interview Survey	To serve as the principal source of information on the health of the civilian noninstitutionalized population of the United States	Children aged 0–17 years	http://www.cdc.gov/nchs/nhis.htm
National Health and Nutrition Examination Survey	To assess the health and nutritional status of adults and children in the United States, through a combination of interviews and physical examinations	Interview surveys of children aged 0–17; hearing examinations of youth 12–17 years	http://www.cdc.gov/nchs/nhanes.htm
National Survey of Children's Health	To examine the physical and emotional health of children	Children aged 0–17 years	http://www.cdc.gov/nchs/slaits/nsch.htm

Source: GAO analysis of HHS surveys.
a For the purposes of our analysis.

We determined that the data were sufficiently reliable for our purposes. Because the survey data were collected using generalizable, probability samples, this sample is only one of a large number of samples that might have been selected. Since each sample could provide different estimates, we have used 95 percent confidence intervals to show the precision of our results. All percentage estimates used in this report have 95 percent confidence intervals of within plus or minus 4 percentage points, unless otherwise noted.

To identify factors associated with the development of language and literacy for deaf and hard of hearing children, we spoke to a variety of national experts, representing educators, parents, and the deaf community, and solicited written comments from a variety of national organizations representing a spectrum of views on deaf education (see table 4).

Table 4. Organizations Interviewed or Providing Written Input

Organization
Alexander Graham Bell Association for the Deaf and Hard of Hearing
National Association of the Deaf
American Society for Deaf Children
National Cued Speech Association
Convention of American Instructors of the Deaf
Registry of Interpreters for the Deaf
National Association of State Directors of Special Education
Conference of Educational Administrators of Schools and Programs for the Deaf
American Speech-Language-Hearing Association
The Laurent Clerc National Deaf Education Center at Gallaudet University
Center for ASL/English Bilingual Education and Research
Hands & Voices
The Association of College Educators-Deaf and Hard of Hearing
American Academy of Audiology

Source: GAO.

We searched numerous databases—including the Education Resources Information Center, the Cumulative Index to Nursing and Allied Health Literature, Electronics Collections Online, ProQuest, and numerous social science and medical literature databases on the Dialog platform—in order to identify recent studies on factors that have been shown to promote language and literacy development for deaf and hard of hearing children. We also consulted with national experts to identify relevant studies. As a result, we identified 159 studies published from 2005 through 2010. We limited the scope of our work by looking at studies that met the following criteria: (1)

original research published since 2005, (2) based in the United States, (3) included five or more participants, and (4) related to a single disability.

Through further review, we found that 26 published studies fell within our scope. Therefore, our results are not an exhaustive or historical treatment of the topic. We conducted detailed reviews of these 26 studies. Our reviews entailed an assessment of each study's research methodology, including its research design, and analytic techniques, as well as a summary of each study's major findings and conclusions. We also assessed the extent to which each study's data and methods support its findings and conclusions.

To identify the challenges that exist to providing appropriate interventions for deaf and hard of hearing children, we reviewed relevant federal laws and regulations for the Early Hearing Detection and Intervention program and the Individuals with Disabilities Education Act (IDEA), and interviewed federal officials responsible for administering these programs. We also spoke to a variety of national organizations and conducted site visits to Colorado, Massachusetts, and Washington state to learn more about the experiences educators and others have had with educational and other services for deaf and hard of hearing children. We selected these states because they vary in terms of the percentage of deaf and hard of hearing children educated in regular classrooms, the educational focus of their state school for the deaf,[1] and their geography. During these visits, we solicited input from a variety of groups and individuals, including state agencies responsible for overseeing IDEA Part C and Part B programs, school district and school administrators, and teachers. We visited a variety of schools encompassing differences in setting (residential, regional programs, children in self-contained classrooms, and children in regular classrooms) and mode of communication (sign language and auditory or oral). In addition, we interviewed 28 parents of deaf and hard of hearing students during our site visits to learn about their experiences and the challenges they face. Local organizations within the states we visited organized meetings of parents who volunteered to meet with us.

We conducted this performance audit from March 2010 to May 2011 in accordance with generally accepted government auditing standards. Those standards require that we plan and perform the audit to obtain sufficient, appropriate evidence to provide a reasonable basis for our findings and conclusions based on our audit objectives. We believe that the evidence obtained provides a reasonable basis for our findings and conclusions based on our audit objectives.

APPENDIX II:
SUMMARY OF KEY PROVISIONS
OF IDEA PART C AND PART B PROGRAMS

	Part C	Part B
Who is eligible for services?	An infant or toddler with a disability, under 3 years of age, who is experiencing a developmental delay or has a diagnosed condition that has a high probability of resulting in a developmental delay.	A child, aged 3–21, with a disability that falls into at least 1 of 10 categories, including hearing impairments, that adversely affects the child's educational performance, and as a resultis determined to require special education services.[a]
What is included in a child's individualized family service plan or individualized education program?	An individualized family service plan should include, among other things, a written assessment of the child's development, acknowledgment of the family's priorities, measurable outcomes and results for the child, and the specific early intervention services to be provided.	An individualized education program should include, among other things, a written assessment of the child's level of performance and academic achievement; measurable annualgoals, including academic goals; and the special education services and accommodations to be provided.
Where does a child receive services?	To the maximum extent appropriate, early intervention services should be provided in a child's natural environments, including the home, and community settings where children without disabilities participate.	Under the principle of least restrictive environment, to the maximum extent appropriate, children with disabilities should be educated with children who are not disabled.

Source: GAO analysis of IDEA, as amended, and implementing regulations found at 34 C.F.R. Part 303 (Part C) and 34 C.F.R. Part 300 (Part B).

[a] The 10 categories are intellectual disabilities, hearing impairments (including deafness), speech or language impairments, visual impairments (including blindness), serious emotional disturbance, orthopedic impairments, autism, traumatic brain injury, other health impairments, and specific learning disabilities.

APPENDIX III:
NATIONAL SURVEY ESTIMATES
OF HEARING LOSS FOR CHILDREN AGED 0–17

Survey	Years	Survey question	Percentage of children, Aged 0–11, experiencing at least a little trouble hearing or told they had hearing roblems	Percentage of children, Aged 12–17, experiencing at least a little trouble hearing or told they had hearing problems
National Health and Nutrition Examination Survey	2005–2008	Which statement best describes the sample child's hearing (without a hearing aid)? Would you say {your/his/her} hearing is good, excellent, that {you have/he has} a little or moderate trouble, a lot of trouble, or {are you/is s/he} deaf?	3.3%	5.3%
National Health Interview Survey	2008–2009	Which statement best describes {the sample child's} hearing without a hearing aid: Excellent, good, a little trouble hearing, moderate trouble, a lot of trouble, or is {the child} deaf?	2	2.5
National Survey of Children's Health	2007	Has a doctor or other health care provider ever told you that {the sample child} had hearing problems?	2.9	3.1

Source: GAO analysis of HHS surveys.

End Notes

[1] The phrases "deaf and hard of hearing" and "children with hearing loss" are used interchangeably throughout the report.

[2] Carol Bloomquist Traxler, "The Stanford Achievement test, 9th Edition: National Norming and Performance Standards for Deaf and Hard-of-Hearing Students," *Journal of Deaf Studies and Deaf Education*, vol. 5, no. 4 (fall 2000): 337–48.

[3] Experts include the Centers for Disease Control and Prevention (CDC), American Speech-Language-Hearing Association, Boys Town National Research Hospital, and Johns Hopkins Medicine. CDC also identifies a fourth type of hearing loss—Auditory Neuropathy Spectrum Disorder, where damage to the inner ear or hearing nerve prevents sound that enters the ear normally from being easily understood by the brain.

[4] The American Speech-Language-Hearing Association cites the following hearing loss classification system, with loss measured in decibels (dB HL): normal hearing loss falls from negative 10 to 15 dB HL, slight loss from 16 to 25 dB HL, mild loss from 26 to 40 dB HL, moderate loss from 41 to 55 dB HL, moderately severe loss from 56 to 70 dB HL, severe loss from 71 to 90 dB HL, and profound loss of 91 dB HL or more. According to the Centers for Disease Control and Prevention, a person with mild hearing loss may hear some speech sounds but find soft sounds difficult to hear whereas someone with profound hearing loss will not hear any speech and only very loud sounds.

[5] Testimony of James F. Battey Jr., M.D., Ph.D., Director, National Institute on Deafness and Other Communication Disorders, before the Subcommittee on Labor, Health and Human Services, Education, and Related Agencies, U.S. Senate Committee on Appropriations (Mar. 26, 2007).

[6] Other assistive technologies, such as an FM system, can help deaf and hard of hearing children communicate in the classroom by sending sound from someone speaking into a microphone to a person wearing the receiver, and can be used in conjunction with hearing aids.

[7] Bone-anchored hearing aids may be used by children who are unable to wear a hearing aid in or behind the ear.

[8] 42 U.S.C. § 280g-1. CDC was appropriated about $10.9 million for EHDI in fiscal year 2009. The same year, HRSA's hearing screening and intervention program was funded at $19 million.

[9] The committee is composed of members of the Alexander Graham Bell Association for the Deaf and Hard of Hearing, the American Academy of Pediatrics, the American Academy of Audiology, the American Academy of Otolaryngology-Head and Neck Surgery, the American Speech-Language-Hearing Association, the Council on Education of the Deaf, and the Directors of Speech and Hearing Programs in State Health and Welfare Agencies.

[10] According to the CDC, the agency does not establish criteria for passing the hearing screening.

[11] Early Hearing Detection and Intervention Act of 2010, Pub. L. No. 111-337, 124 Stat. 3588. The program also aims to develop efficient models to ensure that newborns and infants who are identified with a hearing loss through screening receive follow-up by a qualified health care provider. The EHDI law was first enacted as part of the Departments of Labor, Health and Human Services, and Education Fiscal Year 2000 Appropriations Act, Pub. L. No. 106-113, Appendix D, Title VI, 113 Stat. 1501, 1501A-276 (1999) and was subsequently added as amendment to the Public Health Service Act by section 702 of the Children's Health Act of 2000, Pub. L. No. 106-310, Div. A, Title VII, 114 Stat. 1101, 1120.

[12] IDEA was originally enacted as the Education for All Handicapped Children Act, Pub. L. No. 94-142, 89 Stat. 773.

[13] Individuals with Disabilities Education Improvement Act of 2004, Pub. L. No. 108-446, 118 Stat. 2647. IDEA, as amended, is codified at 20 U.S.C. § 1400 et seq.

[14] In fiscal year 2008, the Part C program was funded at $436 million.

[15] In fiscal year 2008, the Part B program was funded at $10.95 billion.

[16] In addition to IDEA, other laws support the educational needs of children with disabilities, including children who are deaf or hard of hearing. Section 504 of the Rehabilitation Act of 1973 (Section 504) prohibits entities that receive federal financial assistance, including public schools, from discriminating against otherwise qualified individuals with disabilities. Title II of the Americans with Disabilities Act of 1990, as amended, prohibits discrimination on the basis of disability by public entities, including public schools, regardless of whether they receive federal financial assistance. In general, Section 504 and Title II requirements are similar.

[17] Education requires state Part C programs to report on, among other things, the percentage of children exiting Part C who receive timely transition planning to support the child's transition to preschool and other community services by the age of 3. Transition planning includes documentation of appropriate transition steps and services for a child, as well as notification of school districts and a transition conference for children potentially eligible for Part B services. Part B programs are required to report to Education on the percentage of children referred by Part C prior to age 3, who are found eligible for Part B, and who have an individualized education program developed and implemented by their third birthdays.

[18] 20 U.S.C. § 1436 and 34 C.F.R. § 303.342 and § 303.343.

[19] 20 U.S.C. § 1414(d)(1) and 34 C.F.R. § 300.321 and § 300.324.

[20] States must also include procedural safeguards in their programs, such as a right to due process hearings and the right to appeal to federal district court.

[21] These data represent the 50 states only. More than 79,000 deaf and hard of hearing children in the 50 states, the District of Columbia, schools of the Bureau of Indian Education, and the U.S. territories received IDEA Part B services as of fall 2008.

[22] This statistic represents prevalence in the 45 states for which data were available. Alabama, California, Georgia, Nevada, and New York were not included in this analysis.

[23] Infants may be screened for hearing loss more than once; for infants who received multiple screenings, this statistic is based on the results of their most recent screening test.

[24] The families of most infants without a documented diagnosis could not be contacted or were unresponsive (about 82 percent), while other infants had a diagnosis in process (about 9 percent), died or had a parent who refused further testing (about 5 percent), or were nonresidents or moved out of state (about 4 percent).

[25] Pub. L. No. 111-337, § 2, 124 Stat. 3588 (codified at 42 U.S.C. 280g-1(a)(3)).

[26] The most recent year for which hearing test data are available for children in this age range is 1994, when data were collected on children aged 6 to 19. Although existing federal hearing screening and testing programs do not currently cover children of all ages, states may mandate hearing tests for these children. For example, according to the Colorado Department of Education, Colorado requires that children in kindergarten and grades 1–3, 5, 7, and 9 are tested for hearing loss.

[27] The surveys include the National Health Interview Survey (NHIS), National Survey of Children's Health (NSCH), and National Health and Nutrition Examination Survey (NHANES) household interview data. For NHIS and NSCH, a responsible adult, such as a parent or guardian who is knowledgeable about a child's health status, served as the survey respondent. For NHANES, an adult reported information on behalf of children younger than the age of 16.

[28] The National Health and Nutrition Examination Survey is used to assess the health and nutritional status of children and adults in the United States through a combination of interviews and physical examinations. For the purposes of examining data on children, we limited our analysis to 12–17 year olds only. See appendix I for more information.

[29] An estimated 99 percent of 12–17 year olds had hearing ranging from normal to mild loss and less than an estimated 1 percent experienced severe or profound loss.

[30] For poverty status, we compared 12–17 year olds from families with income below 200 percent of federal poverty guidelines and at or above 200 percent of the guidelines. For race, we compared non-Hispanic white children and non-Hispanic African-American children. We selected these races due to the limited sample sizes available by race.

[31] Marianne Ahlgren, Julie Jodoin-Krauzyk, Mary Jane Johnson, Deborah Topol, Richard Tucker, and Betty Vohr, "Early Language Outcomes of Early-Identified Infants With Permanent Hearing Loss at 12 to 16 Months of Age," *Pediatrics*, vol. 122, no. 3 (2008).

[32] Carol McDonald Connor, Holly K. Craig, Krista Heavner, Stephen W. Raudenbush, and Teresa A. Zwolan, "The Age at Which Young Deaf Children Receive Cochlear Implants and Their Vocabulary and Speech-Production Growth: Is There an Added Value for Early Implantation?" *Ear and Hearing*, vol. 27, no. 6 (2006).

[33] Amy R. Lederberg and Patricia E. Spencer, "Word-Learning Abilities in Deaf and Hard-of-Hearing Preschoolers: Effect of Lexicon Size and Language Modality," *Journal of Deaf Studies and Deaf Education*, vol. 14, no. 1 (2009).

[34] For the committee's policy, see *Pediatrics*, vol. 120, no. 4 (2007).

[35] Deaf Students Education Services; Policy Guidance, 57 Fed. Reg. 49,274 (Oct. 30, 1992).

[36] National Association of State Directors of Special Education, Inc., *Meeting the Needs of Students Who Are Deaf or Hard of Hearing: Educational Services Guidelines* (Alexandria, Va, July 2006).

[37] 2008 CDC EHDI Hearing Screening & Follow-up Survey. These data were reported from 44 states.

[38] National Center for Hearing Assessment and Management, *The Impact of Privacy Regulations: How EHDI, Part C, & Health Providers Can Ensure that Children & Families Get Needed Services* (Logan, Utah, May 2008).

[39] The EIPA test was developed by the Boys Town National Research Hospital and uses skilled deaf and hearing raters to provide diagnostic services for individual interpreters, states, educational settings and school districts. RID considers a score of 4.0 or higher on the EIPA as qualifying for RID certification.

End Notes for Appendix I

[1] Massachusetts does not have a state school for the deaf.

In: Child Health Care Support Programs ...   ISBN: 978-1-61470-970-1
Editors: W. Y. and X. Wen   © 2012 Nova Science Publishers, Inc.

Chapter 2

ORAL HEALTH: EFFORTS UNDER WAY TO IMPROVE CHILDREN'S ACCESS TO DENTAL SERVICES, BUT SUSTAINED ATTENTION NEEDED TO ADDRESS ONGOING CONCERNS[*]

United States Government Accountability Office

WHY GAO DID THIS STUDY

The Children's Health Insurance Program Reauthorization Act of 2009 (CHIPRA) required GAO to study children's access to dental care. GAO assessed (1) the extent to which dentists participate in Medicaid and the Children's Health Insurance Program (CHIP) and federal efforts to help families find participating dentists; (2) data on access for Medicaid and CHIP children in different states and in managed care; (3) federal efforts to improve access in underserved areas; and (4) how states and other countries have used mid-level dental providers to improve children's access. To do this, GAO (1) examined state reported dentist participation and the Department of Health and Human Services's (HHS) Insure Kids Now Web site for all 50 states and the

---

[*] This is an edited, reformatted and augmented version of the United States Government Accountability Office publication, Report to Congressional Committees GAO-11-96, dated November 2010.

District of Columbia and called a non-representative sample of dentists in four states; (2) reviewed national data on provision of Medicaid dental services and use of managed care; (3) interviewed HHS officials and assessed certain HHS dental programs; and (4) interviewed officials in eight states and four countries on the use of mid-level and other dental providers.

WHAT GAO RECOMMENDS

GAO recommends that HHS take steps to improve its Insure Kids Now Web site and ensure that states gather complete and reliable data on Medicaid and CHIP dental services provided under managed care. HHS agreed with the recommendations, citing specific actions it would take.

WHAT GAO FOUND

Obtaining dental care for children in Medicaid and CHIP remains a challenge, as many states reported that most dentists in their state treat few or no Medicaid or CHIP patients. And, while HHS's Insure Kids Now Web site— which provides information on dentists who serve children enrolled in Medicaid and CHIP—has the potential to help families find dentists to treat their children, GAO found problems, such as incomplete and inaccurate information, that limited the Web site's ability to do so. For example, to test the accuracy of the information posted on the Web site, GAO called 188 dentists listed on the Web site in low-income urban and rural areas in four states representing varied geographic areas and levels of dental managed care and with high numbers of children in Medicaid. Of these 188 contacts, 26 had wrong or disconnected phone numbers listed, 23 were not taking new Medicaid or CHIP patients, and 47 were either not in practice or no longer performing routine exams.

Although improved since 2001, available national data show that in 2008, less than 37 percent of children in Medicaid received any dental services under that program and that several states reported rates of 30 percent or less. Further, although some data indicate that children in Medicaid managed care may receive less dental care than other children, comprehensive and reliable data on dental services under managed care continue to be unavailable despite long-standing concerns. Although HHS has not required states to report information on the provision of dental services under CHIP, CHIPRA requires states to begin reporting this information for fiscal year 2010.

Two programs that provide dental services to children and adults in underserved areas—HHS's Health Center and National Health Service Corps (NHSC) programs—have reported increases in the number of dentists and dental hygienists practicing in underserved areas, but the effect of recent initiatives to increase federal support for these and other oral health programs is not yet known. Despite these increases, both health centers and the NHSC program report continued need for additional dentists and other dental providers to treat children and adults in underserved areas.

Mid-level dental providers—providers who may perform intermediate restorative services, such as drilling and filling teeth, under remote supervision of a dentist—are in limited use in the United States. The only currently practicing mid-level dental providers in the United States serve Alaska Natives. Efforts to supplement the U.S. dental workforce with midlevel and other types of providers are under way. GAO interviewed officials from eight states with varied state laws related to dental providers. Some states have made efforts to increase children's access by reimbursing dental hygienists and primary care physicians for providing certain dental services. Some countries have long-standing programs that use mid-level dental providers, also known as dental therapists, who the countries report have improved children's access to dental services.

ABBREVIATIONS

ASTDD	Association of State and Territorial Dental Directors
CHIP	Children's Health Insurance Program
CHIPRA	Children's Health Insurance Program Reauthorization Act of 2009
CMS	Centers for Medicare & Medicaid Services
EPSDT	Early and Periodic Screening, Diagnostic, and Treatment
FTE	full-time equivalent
HHS	Department of Health and Human Services
HIV	human immunodeficiency virus
HPSA	health professional shortage area
HRSA	Health Resources and Services Administration
NHSC	National Health Service Corps
OIG	Office of Inspector General
PPACA	Patient Protection and Affordable Care Act

November 30, 2010
The Honorable Max Baucus, Chairman
The Honorable Charles E. Grassley
Ranking Member, Committee on Finance
United States Senate

The Honorable Henry A. Waxman, Chairman
The Honorable Joe Barton, Ranking Member
Committee on Energy and Commerce
House of Representatives

Since 2000, our reports as well as reports by the Surgeon General, congressional committees, and oral health researchers have underscored the high rates of dental disease and the challenges of providing dental services to children living in underserved areas and in low-income families. In particular, children with health care coverage under two joint federal-state programs for low-income children—Medicaid and the Children's Health Insurance Program (CHIP)—often have difficulty finding dental care even though dental services are a covered benefit.[1] For example we reported in 2000 that low-income and minority populations— including children in Medicaid and CHIP—had a disproportionately high level of dental disease. In a related report, we found that the major factor contributing to the low use of dental services among low-income persons was finding dentists to treat them, even in areas where dental care for the rest of the population was generally available.[2] We also reported that dentists generally cited low payment rates, administrative requirements, and patient issues such as frequently missed appointments as reasons why they did not treat Medicaid patients. In 2008, we reported that the situation was largely unchanged. National survey data showed dental disease remained a significant problem for children in Medicaid—we estimated that 6.5 million children had untreated tooth decay and rates of dental disease among children in Medicaid had not decreased over time.[3] National surveys also showed that only one in three children in Medicaid had visited a dentist in the prior year, compared to more than half of privately insured children. In a 2009 survey of state Medicaid programs, we found that identifying a dentist who accepted Medicaid remained the most frequently reported barrier to children seeking dental services. We also found that, of the 21 states that provided Medicaid dental services under managed care arrangements, more than half reported that managed care organizations in their states did not meet any, or only met some, of the state's dental access standards.[4]

Since 2009, a number of actions have been taken to address these challenges. For example, to help families find a dentist to treat children covered by Medicaid and CHIP, the Children's Health Insurance Program Reauthorization Act of 2009 (CHIPRA) required the Department of Health and Human Services (HHS) to post on its Insure Kids Now Web site a current and accurate list of dentists participating in state Medicaid and CHIP programs.[5] In April 2010, HHS launched a departmentwide oral health initiative to expand oral health services, education, and research, including promoting access to oral health care and the effective delivery of services to underserved populations.

CHIPRA also required that we study and report on various aspects of children's access to dental services.[6] This report discusses (1) the extent to which dentists participate in Medicaid and CHIP, and federal efforts t o help families find dentists to treat children in these programs; (2) what is known about access for Medicaid and CHIP children in different states and in managed care; (3) federal efforts under way to improve access to dental services by children in underserved areas; and (4) how states and other countries have used mid-level dental providers to improve children's access to dental services.

To examine the extent to which dentists participate in Medicaid and CHIP, and federal efforts to help families find dentists to treat children in these programs, we (1) analyzed survey responses from states regarding dentists' participation in Medicaid and CHIP, gathered by the Association of State and Territorial Dental Directors (ASTDD), and (2) evaluated information posted on HHS's Insure Kids Now Web site about the dentists participating in Medicaid and CHIP. Specifically, we reviewed the information on the Web site for all 50 states and the District of Columbia to evaluate whether certain data elements specified as required in guidance from the Centers for Medicare & Medicaid Services (CMS)—the HHS agency that administers Medicaid at the federal level—were posted and whether the Web site was usable for a family seeking to identify a dentist for a child covered by Medicaid or CHIP. We also tested the accuracy of information posted to the Web site by calling a nongeneralizeable sample of 188 dentists' offices in low-income urban and rural areas in 4 states.[7] We also reviewed relevant academic and association research on dental services for children with special health care needs.

To evaluate what is known about access for Medicaid and CHIP children in different states and in managed care, we reviewed documents and interviewed officials from CMS. We also (1) analyzed survey responses from states on the use of dental managed care in Medicaid, gathered by the

American Dental Association; and (2) examined annual state reports on the provision of dental services under the Medicaid Early and Periodic Screening, Diagnostic, and Treatment (EPSDT) benefit.[8]

To identify federal efforts to improve children's access to dental services in underserved areas, we focused on two programs administered by HHS's Health Resources and Services Administration (HRSA)—the Health Center program and the National Health Service Corps (NHSC) program— designed, in part, to support the provision of dental services in underserved areas. We also examined information regarding other recent efforts to improve access to care for children in underserved areas, including funding made available by the American Recovery and Reinvestment Act of 2009 (Recovery Act) and the Patient Protection and Affordable Care Act (PPACA).[9]

To determine how states have used mid-level dental providers to improve access to dental services for children, we examined laws, regulations, and practices related to mid-level and other dental providers and interviewed federal officials as well as officials in 8 selected states—Alabama, Alaska, California, Colorado, Minnesota, Mississippi, Oregon, and Washington— that have varying degrees of education, supervision, and scope-of-practice requirements for dental providers.[10] We selected these states based on responses we obtained to a standard set of questions posed to oral health researchers, professional associations, and advocacy groups regarding states that use mid-level and other dental providers to expand access to dental services. We visited Alaska to interview state and tribal officials on efforts to expand access for Alaska Natives through the use of mid-level dental providers. To determine how other countries have used mid-level dental providers to improve access to dental services for children, we examined documents and interviewed officials from four countries — Australia, Canada, New Zealand, and the United Kingdom. See appendix I for additional information on our scope and methodology.

We conducted this performance audit from August 2009 through November 2010 in accordance with generally accepted government auditing standards. Those standards require that we plan and perform the audit to obtain sufficient, appropriate evidence to provide a reasonable basis for our findings and conclusions based on our audit objectives. We believe the evidence obtained provides a reasonable basis for our findings and conclusions based on our audit objectives.

BACKGROUND

High rates of dental disease and low utilization of dental services by children in low-income families and the challenge of finding dentists to treat them are long-standing concerns. In 2000, the Surgeon General reported that tooth decay is the most common chronic childhood disease and described what the report called the silent epidemic of oral disease affecting the nation's poor children.[11] Left untreated, the pain and infections caused by tooth decay may lead to problems in eating, speaking, and learning. Tooth decay is almost completely preventable and the pain, dysfunction, or on extremely rare occasions, even death, resulting from dental disease can be avoided. The American Academy of Pediatric Dentistry recommends that each child see a dentist when his or her first tooth erupts and no later than the child's first birthday, with subsequent visits occurring at 6-month intervals or more frequently if recommended by a dentist.

Recognizing the importance of good oral health, HHS established oral health goals as part of its Healthy People 2000 and 2010 initiatives.[12] One objective of Healthy People 2010 was to increase the proportion of low-income children and adolescents under the age of 19 who receive any preventive dental service in the past year—including examination, x-ray, fluoride application, cleaning, or sealant application (a plastic material placed on molars to reduce the risk of tooth decay)—from 20 percent in 1996 to 66 percent in 2010.

Federal Programs that Promote Dental Services for Children

Medicaid, a joint federal and state program that provides health care coverage for certain low-income individuals and families, provided health coverage for over 30 million children under 21 in fiscal year 2008.[13] States operate their Medicaid programs within broad federal requirements and may contract with managed care organizations to provide Medicaid medical and dental benefits. Under federal law, state Medicaid programs must provide dental services, including diagnostic, preventive, and related treatment services for all eligible Medicaid enrollees under age 21 under the program's EPSDT benefit.

Federal law also requires states to report annually on the provision of EPSDT services, including dental services, for children in Medicaid. The annual EPSDT participation report, Form CMS-416 (hereafter called the CMS

416), is the agency's primary tool for gathering data on the provision of dental services to children in state Medicaid programs. It captures data on the number of children who received any dental services, a preventive dental service, or a dental treatment service each year. Information on the CMS 416 is used to calculate a state's dental utilization rate—the percentage of children eligible for EPSDT who received any dental service in a given year.

CHIP, which is also a joint federal and state program, expanded health coverage to children—approximately 7.7 million children in fiscal year 2009—whose families have incomes that are low, but not low enough to qualify for Medicaid.[14] States can administer their CHIP programs as (1) an expansion of their Medicaid programs, (2) a stand-alone program, or (3) a combination of Medicaid expansion and stand-alone. Although states have flexibility in establishing their CHIP benefit package, all states covered some dental services in 2009, according to CMS officials, though benefits varied. Children in CHIP programs that are administered as expansions of Medicaid programs are entitled to the same dental services under the EPSDT benefit as children in Medicaid.

CHIPRA expanded federal requirements for state CHIP programs to cover dental services. Specifically, CHIPRA required states to cover dental services in their CHIP programs beginning in October 2009 and gave states authority to use benchmark plans to define the benefit package or to supplement children's private health insurance with a dental coverage plan financed through CHIP.[15] CHIPRA also required states to submit annual reports to CMS on the provision of dental and other services—similar to information provided by state Medicaid programs each year on their CMS 416 reports.[16] States were previously required to submit annual CHIP reports, although these reports did not contain detailed information on the provision of dental services as required for Medicaid on the CMS 416.

To make it easier for families to find dentists to treat children covered by Medicaid and CHIP, CHIPRA also required that HHS post "a current and accurate list of all such dentists and providers within each State that provide dental services to children" under Medicaid or CHIP on its Insure Kids Now Web site. CHIPRA required the Secretary of HHS to post this list on the Web site by August 4, 2009, and ensure that the list is updated at least quarterly.[17] In June 2009, CMS issued guidance specifying certain data elements required for each dentist listed on the Insure Kids Now Web site—including the dentist's name, address, telephone number, and specialty; whether the dentist accepts new Medicaid or CHIP patients; and whether the dentist can accommodate patients with special needs. HHS posts listings on the Insure

Kids Now Web site by state and in some cases provides a link to such a list on an individual state's or managed care organization's Web site.

To address the need for health services in underserved areas of the country, HHS's HRSA administers programs that support the provision of dental and other medical services in underserved areas. For example, under HRSA's Health Center program, health centers—which must be located in federally designated medically underserved areas or serve a federally designated medically underserved population—are required to provide pediatric dental screenings and preventive dental services, as well as emergency medical referrals, which may also result in the provision of dental services.[18] Health centers must accept Medicaid and CHIP patients and treat everyone regardless of their ability to pay. HHS reported that in fiscal year 2009, over 1,100 health center grantees operated over 7,900 service delivery sites in every state and the District of Columbia, and provided health care services, including dental services, to approximately 19 million patients, about one-third of whom were children.

Another HRSA program, NHSC, offers scholarships and educational loan repayment for clinicians who agree to practice in underserved areas.[19] NHSC awards scholarships to students entering certain health professions training programs, including dentistry, who agree to practice in underserved areas when their training is completed. NHSC also provides educational loan repayment for health care providers, including dentists and dental hygienists, who have completed their training and can begin serving in a shortage area. HRSA designates geographic areas, population groups, and facilities as dental health professional shortage areas (HPSAs) for purposes of placing dentists and dental hygienists through the NHSC program. These designations are based, in part, on the number of dentists in an area compared to the area's population.[20] As of July 13, 2010, HRSA reported that there were 4,377 dental HPSAs in the United States[21] and estimated that it would take 7,008 full-time equivalent (FTE) dentists to remove these designations.[22] To be eligible for a NHSC provider, a site must be located in a HPSA of greatest shortage and meet other requirements, such as accepting Medicaid and CHIP patients and treating everyone regardless of their ability to pay.[23] Providers can then choose where they wish to serve from a list of eligible sites, although providers who have received scholarships are limited to a narrower list of higher priority vacancies.[24] According to HRSA, about half of all NHSC providers, which include dentists and hygienists, practice in health centers.

Dental Services and Dental Providers

Dental services cover a broad array of specialized procedures, from routine exams to complex restorative procedures. For this report, we grouped dental services into five main categories: (1) supportive, (2) preventive, (3) basic restorative, (4) intermediate restorative, and (5) advanced restorative dental procedures (see table 1).

Table 1. Categories of Dental Services and Examples of Dental Procedures

Supportive	Preventive	Basic restorative	Intermediate restorative	Advanced restorative
• Preparing a patient to be examined by a dentist • Passing instruments to a dentist	• Examination and assessment • Counseling • Cleaning above and below gum line • Fluoride application • Sealant placementa	• Temporary fillings • Smoothing an existing restoration • Administration of local anesthetic	• Tooth preparation (drilling) • Tooth restoration (filling) • Tooth extractions	• Periodontal treatment (gums) • Endodontic treatment (root canals)

Source: GAO.

[a] Dental sealants are plastic material that are commonly applied to the chewing surfaces of back teeth to reduce the risk of decay.

While a provider's specific scope of practice may vary by state, types of dental providers who may provide some or all of these services include:

- Dentists, who may perform the full range of dental procedures.[25]
- Mid-level dental providers, often dental therapists, who may perform preventive, basic restorative, and intermediate restorative dental procedures under remote supervision of a licensed dentist.

- Dental hygienists, who generally perform preventive procedures, such as tooth cleaning, oral health education, and fluoride applications, as well as basic restorative procedures in certain states, under various supervisory agreements with a dentist.
- Dental assistants, who may provide supportive services and in some states certain preventive and basic restorative procedures under on-site supervision of a dentist.
- Primary health care providers (such as physicians and nurse practitioners) who may also perform certain preventive dental procedures, such as applying fluoride varnish, to children in some states.

Dental therapists, dental hygienists, and dental assistants work under various supervisory arrangements with a dentist. The type of supervision required for these providers may vary depending upon the state and the type of service provided. For this report, we categorized dental supervision as on-site, remote with prior knowledge and consent, remote with consultative agreement, or no supervision (see table 2).

Table 2. Types of Supervision for Other Dental Providers

Supervision type	Description
On-site supervision	The dentist must be on-site when the dental provider performs services and examines the patient at any point before, during, or after the dental services are provided.
Remote supervision with prior knowledge and consent	The dentist may be off-site but must have prior knowledge of and consent to the procedures, in some cases through a treatment plan.
Remote supervision with consultative agreement	The dentist may be off-site but maintain a consultative role, for example through a signed collaborative agreement with another type of dental provider.
No supervision	Dental provider may perform services without dentists' supervision.

Source: GAO.

Note: This table presents examples of the type of supervisory arrangements that may exist between dentists and other dental providers, such as dental therapists and dental hygienists.

FOR CHILDREN IN MEDICAID AND CHIP, FINDING A DENTIST REMAINS A CHALLENGE, AND HHS'S WEB SITE TO HELP LOCATE PARTICIPATING DENTISTS WAS NOT ALWAYS COMPLETE OR ACCURATE

States continue to report low participation by dentists in Medicaid and CHIP. While HHS's Insure Kids Now Web site—which provides information on dentists who serve children enrolled in Medicaid and CHIP—has potential to help families find a dentist to treat children in these programs, we found problems such as incomplete or inaccurate information that limit its ability to do so.

States Report Low Dentist Participation in Medicaid and CHIP, and Children with Special Health Care Needs Face Particular Difficulties

While comprehensive nationwide data do not exist, available data suggest that problems with low dentist participation in Medicaid and CHIP persist. Additionally, among dentists who do participate in Medicaid, many may place limits on the number of Medicaid patients that they will treat. Most states responding to a 2009 ASTDD survey[26] reported low participation among dentists, although not all states responded completely. Our analysis shows that 25 of 39 states reported that fewer than half of the dentists in their states treated any Medicaid patients during the previous year.[27] Only one of 41 states reported that more than half of the state's dentists saw 100 or more Medicaid patients during the previous year (see table 3). Fewer states responding to the 2009 ASTDD survey provided data on dentists' participation in CHIP separately from data on participation in Medicaid and CHIP expansions, but the data reported separately for CHIP indicates that dentists' participation in CHIP is also low.

The results of the 2009 ASTDD survey indicating low levels of dentists' participation in Medicaid are consistent with findings we reported in 2000. We reported that 16 of 39 states responding to our inquiry indicated that more than half of the dentists in the state treated any Medicaid patients in 1999, but that none of the states reported that more than half of the dentists treated 100 or more Medicaid patients.[28]

Table 3. State Reported Data on Dentists'
Participation in Medicaid and CHIP

	State officials' responses to 2009 Association of State and Territorial Dental Directors (ASTDD) survey	
Level of Dentist Participation in Medicaid or CHIP	Medicaid or CHIP expansion[a]	CHIP only
States reporting more than half of the dentists in the state treat any patients	14 of 39 states (36%)	4 of 11 states (36%)
States reporting more than half of the dentists in the state treat 100 or more patients	1 of 41 states (2%)	0 of 12 states (0%)

Source: GAO analysis of ASTDD survey data.

Note: This table presents data collected by ASTDD in 2009. ASTDD sent its survey to dental directors in all states and the District of Columbia and received 45 responses. Information collected was for fiscal year 2008 (or the most recent available fiscal year).

[a] States have the option of administering their CHIP programs as expansions of their Medicaid programs.

One group of children particularly affected by low levels of dentists' participation in Medicaid and CHIP are children with special health care needs. On its Web site, HRSA's Maternal and Child Health Bureau has defined children with special health care needs as "those who have or are at increased risk for a chronic physical, developmental, behavioral, or emotional condition and who also require health and related services of a type or amount beyond that required by children generally." According to a March 2009 ASTDD evaluation of 17 state oral health programs, the most common barriers to dental services for children with special health care needs include low rates of dentists' participation in Medicaid and CHIP, difficulty locating dentists who accept children with special health care needs who have behavioral challenges, and the high cost of specialized care.[29] Studies have also cited the lack of training for dentists to accommodate children who have special treatment needs.[30] In response to the 2005–2006 National Survey of Children with Special Health Care Needs—a periodic survey sponsored by HRSA's Maternal and Child Health Bureau and carried out by the Centers for Disease Control and Prevention—parents (or guardians) of children with special health care needs reported that unmet dental care was the greatest health care need for these children and reported problems getting dental care at levels that exceeded those of healthy children. Unmet dental care for children with special heath care needs can also vary by diagnosis. For example, a study based on the 2005–2006 National Survey of Children with Special Health Care Needs found that children with Down's Syndrome were about twice as likely to have unmet dental needs as children with asthma.[31] The study also reported that the odds of having unmet dental care needs were 13 times greater for low-income children with more severe special health care needs compared with higher-income children without special health care needs.[32]

Information on HHS's Web Site to Help Locate Participating Dentists Was Not Always Complete or Accurate

To help families locate dentists near them to treat children in Medicaid or CHIP, CHIPRA required HHS to post information on participating dentists on its Insure Kids Now Web site. However, we found problems with the data available through the Web site—specifically that the listings available on the Web site or through links available from the Web site were not always complete and accurate. CHIPRA required HHS to post a current and accurate list of dentists participating in Medicaid or CHIP on the Web site by August 2009 and to ensure that the list is updated at least quarterly. In August 2010, officials from CMS—the agency within HHS responsible for implementation and that established the data elements that states should provide—described the Web site as a "work in progress" and reported that they are continually improving the site. Although we found that improvements were evident over a 6-month period, problems remained. Specifically, we found cases in which information posted on the Web site was not complete, not usable, or not accurate.

- Completeness. Our review of dentist listings for all 50 states and the District of Columbia in November 2009, 3 months after CHIPRA required HHS to post the list of participating dentists, found a variety of problems, including missing or incomplete information on dentists' telephone numbers and addresses, whether dentists accepted new Medicaid or CHIP patients, and whether dentists could accommodate children with special needs. Our second review of dentist listings in April 2010 for these data found some improvements had been made, but that problems with missing or incomplete information continued for some states (see table 4).

**Table 4. Number of States Providing Missing or Incomplete Dentist
Information through HHS's Insure Kids Now Web Site
in November 2009 and April 2010**

Required data element missing or incomplete		Number of States	
		November 2009	April 2010
Medicaid	Missing or incomplete contact information (i.e., name, address, telephone number) for some or all dentists	10	10
	Did not indicate for all dentists whether dentist accepts new patients	34	29
	Did not indicate for all dentists whether dentist can accommodate patients with special needs	40	37
CHIP	Missing or incomplete contact information (i.e., name, address, telephone number) for some or all dentists	17	14
	Did not indicate for all dentists whether dentist accepts new patients	34	29
	Did not indicate for all dentists whether dentist can accommodate patients with special needs	38	36

Source: GAO analysis of HHS's Insure Kids Now Web site for 50 states and the
District of Columbia.

Note: This table presents the results of our review of the information posted on HHS's
Insure Kids Now Web site in November 2009 and April 2010. Specifically, we
examined each state's listing of dentists to determine if certain data elements,
specified in CMS guidance as required, were present for all dentists in all
Medicaid and CHIP programs operated by the state and recorded instances in
which data were missing or incomplete for all or some dentists.

- Usability. In May 2010, we reviewed all state dentist listings on the
  Insure Kids Now Web site to determine whether families of a child in
  Medicaid or CHIP could reasonably use the site to find potential
  dentists near them and found that listings from 25 states and the
  District of Columbia had usability problems that prevented or
  hampered the search for a dentist participating in Medicaid or CHIP.
  For example, menu or search functions for 14 states did not work for a
  program or entire state—with no indication of when functions would
  be restored or how the user could obtain alternate assistance while it
  was unavailable. Other problems we encountered included broken or
  incorrect links (for example, one state link that took the user to an
  unrelated agency in another state) and confusing menus that could
  hinder the search. For example, seven states listed multiple health
  plans with similar names, some containing typographical errors and
  some that produced different provider listings, increasing the

likelihood of selecting the wrong plan and generating an incorrect list of dentists.

- Accuracy. To check the accuracy of information on dentists posted on the Insure Kids Now Web site, in May 2010 we called the telephone number listed for 188 general dentists shown on HHS's Web site as practicing in selected low-income urban and rural areas in four states[33] and found problems in about half (96) of the listings we checked, including dentists who were not accepting children in Medicaid or CHIP and wrong or disconnected telephone numbers (see table 5). We also asked respondents to tell us what the typical wait time would be for an appointment with the dentists. Of 92 dentists we called that reported that they accepted new Medicaid or CHIP patients under age 19, all but one reported that the wait time was the same for Medicaid or CHIP patients and privately insured patients.[34]

Table 5. Errors in Dentist Listings on HHS's Insure Kids Now Web Site, May 2010

State (number of dentists whose offices we called)	Wrong or disconnected telephone number, percentage (number of errors)	Errors in other posted information,[a] percentage (number of errors)	Not accepting new Medicaid or CHIP children, percentage (number of errors)
California (40)	5% (2)	8% (3)	30% (12)
Georgia (45)	4% (2)	38% (17)	11% (5)
Illinois (56)	36% (20)	36% (20)	4% (2)
Vermont (47)	4% (2)	38% (18)	9% (4)

Source: GAO analysis.

Note: In May 2010, we called the telephone number listed on HHS's Insure Kids Now Web site for 188 dentists in California, Georgia, Illinois, and Vermont—states we selected because they provided variation in geography, use of Medicaid dental managed care, and the number of children covered by Medicaid. Within each state we identified 25 urban dentists and 15 rural dentists to call in the areas with the largest number of children in poverty. For a dentist in a group practice, a single telephone call could yield additional dentists; thus more dentists were called in some states. We accounted for each dentist separately, so an error such as a wrong telephone number for a dental clinic with multiple dentists would account for multiple errors.

[a] Other errors included incorrect addresses (11) or dentists no longer in practice or not providing routine examinations (47).

In addition, while CMS issued guidance requiring states to indicate on the Web site whether a dentist could treat children with special needs, as of August 2010, CMS had not defined what capabilities dentists who serve children with special needs should have, and we found some confusion among dentists' offices regarding their ability to treat these children. For example, several of the dentist offices we called indicated they were unsure whether they could serve children with special needs, while others indicated that they would try to serve them. Of the dentist offices that responded to questions about specific capabilities, nearly all (89 of 95) reported that their offices were wheelchair accessible, but few (6 of 74) reported that they could treat children requiring sedation—although a small number indicated that they would refer the patient to another dentist who could provide sedation.

Finally, we identified one dentist shown on a state's Insure Kids Now listing of dentists treating children enrolled in Medicaid or CHIP who was on HHS's register of excluded providers and should not have been allowed to receive reimbursement from either program.[35] We contacted the dentist's office on May 5, 2010 as part of our review of the accuracy of the information posted on the Web site and the dentist's office confirmed that the dentist was accepting new Medicaid patients. We also contacted the HHS Office of Inspector General (OIG), which administers the HHS exclusion program and HHS-OIG officials confirmed that the dentist had been excluded from participation in the Medicaid program and that the dentist had been reinstated effective May 13, 2010.[36]

STATES REPORT IMPROVEMENT IN THE PROVISION OF DENTAL SERVICES TO CHILDREN IN MEDICAID, BUT DATA TO MONITOR SERVICE PROVISION UNDER CHIP OR MANAGED CARE ARE LIMITED

Although annual state reports on the CMS 416 indicate that the provision of dental services to children in Medicaid nationwide had improved between 2001 and 2008 (the most recent data available at the time of our review), overall utilization rates remained low. In addition, data to measure provision of dental services for some children, such as those in managed care programs or in CHIP, are limited.

STATES REPORT IMPROVEMENT IN THE PROVISION OF DENTAL SERVICES TO CHILDREN IN MEDICAID BETWEEN 2001 AND 2008, BUT UTILIZATION REMAINS LOW

According to data provided by states on annual CMS 416 reports, utilization of dental services among children in Medicaid had improved, but reported utilization rates still varied among states.[37] Nationwide, reported utilization of any Medicaid dental service increased—from 27 percent of children in federal fiscal year 2001 to 36 percent of children in federal fiscal year 2008—but despite this increase, no dental service utilization was reported for nearly two-thirds of Medicaid-enrolled children.[38]

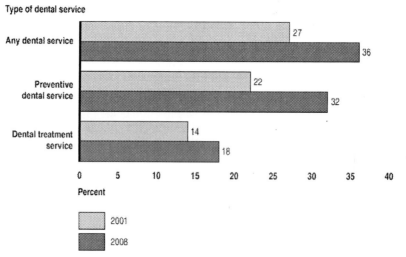

Source: GAO analysis of CMS 416 data.

Note: This figure represents national dental utilization rates calculated from data reported by states in their CMS 416 reports submitted for federal fiscal years 2001 and 2008 on the number of EPSDT eligible Medicaid-enrolled children who received a dental service during the fiscal year. Children enrolled in CHIP programs that are expansions of the states' Medicaid programs are entitled to the Medicaid EPSDT benefit package and are included in the states CMS 416 reports, but are not identified separately as CHIP enrollees.

Figure 1. Comparison of Nationwide Medicaid Dental Utilization Rates for Dental Services for Children, Fiscal Years 2001 and 2008.

Overall, states also reported a higher proportion of children receiving preventive dental services than dental treatment services in both years (see fig. 1).

Although the percentage of children nationwide in Medicaid who received any dental service increased, there continued to be wide variation among states in the percentage of children reported to have received any dental service, including eight states that reported dental utilization rates at 30 percent or less in fiscal year 2008 (see fig. 2).

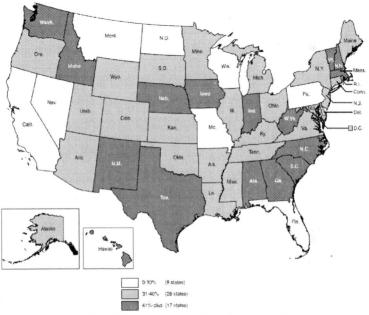

0-30%   (8 states)
31-40%   (26 states)
41%-plus (17 states)

Source: GAO analysis of CMS Form 416 data; Map Resources (map).

Note: This figure represents dental utilization rates calculated from data reported by states in their fiscal year 2008 CMS 416 reports (the most recent available at the time of our review) on the number of EPSDT-eligible Medicaid-enrolled children who received any dental service during the fiscal year. Nationwide, 36 percent of children in Medicaid received any dental service in fiscal year 2008. Children enrolled in CHIP programs that are expansions of the states' Medicaid programs are entitled to the Medicaid EPSDT benefit package and are included in the states' CMS 416 reports, but are not identified separately as CHIP enrollees. Dental utilization rates are rounded to the nearest whole percentage.

Figure 2. Percentage of Children in Medicaid Receiving Any Dental Service, Fiscal Year 2008.

There was also wide variation among states in utilization rates for preventive and dental treatment services—see appendix II for a complete list of the utilization rates for any dental service, preventive dental services, and dental treatment services reported by states in their fiscal year 2008 CMS 416 reports.

For Children in Managed Care and Children in CHIP, Data on the Provision of Dental Services Are Limited

Comprehensive and reliable data on dental utilization by children in Medicaid managed care programs and children in CHIP are not available. States do not distinguish between fee-for-service and managed care programs when reporting annual Medicaid data to CMS (using CMS 416).[39] A comparison of fiscal year 2008 CMS 416 data with available data on the proportion of children in Medicaid managed care in a given state suggests that children in Medicaid managed care plans may have lower dental utilization rates than children in fee-for-service programs. Our analysis of 2008 data on Medicaid managed care penetration rates from the American Dental Association found that 10 states provided dental services predominantly through dental managed care programs.[40] These 10 states reported that 34 percent of children covered by Medicaid received any dental service, compared to 41 percent of children reported by the 33 states that reimbursed exclusively under fee-for-service.

Questions about the provision of Medicaid dental services under managed care compared to fee-for-service payment arrangements are long-standing. In 2007, we reported that CMS had taken steps to improve the CMS 416 data, but that concerns remained about the completeness and sufficiency of the data for purposes of overseeing Medicaid dental services.[41] In particular, we noted that the information could not be used to identify problems with specific delivery methods. Following our report, CMS officials had considered revising the CMS 416 to capture services delivered through managed care; however, as of August 2010, CMS officials did not have any plans to do so.

In addition, national data were not available on the provision of CHIP dental services, although CMS will require improved reporting per CHIPRA in 2011 for dental services provided in 2010. Although states must assess the operation of their CHIP programs each federal fiscal year and report on the results of this assessment,[42] CMS had not required states to include specific information on the provision of CHIP dental services, such as required for

Medicaid dental services in the CMS 416. However, beginning in fiscal year 2010, CHIPRA requires states to include information on CHIP dental services of the type contained in the CMS 416 in their annual CHIP reports and further requires the inclusion of information on the provision of CHIP dental services in managed care programs.[43] According to CMS officials, a CMS work group is developing specific reporting requirements for CHIP dental services provided by states in fiscal year 2010, with first reports due to CMS in 2011.

FEDERAL EFFORTS TO IMPROVE ACCESS TO DENTAL SERVICES FOR CHILDREN IN UNDERSERVED AREAS ARE UNDER WAY, BUT EFFECT IS NOT YET KNOWN

Two HHS programs that provide dental services to children as well as adults in underserved areas—HRSA's Health Center and NHSC programs—have reported increases in the number of dentists and dental hygienists practicing in underserved areas, but the effect of recent initiatives to increase federal support for these and other oral health programs is not yet known. And despite these increases, some gaps may remain. For example, even with recent increases, both health centers and the NHSC program report continued need for additional dentists and dental hygienists to treat children and adults in underserved areas.

Health Center and NHSC Programs Report Recent Increases in the Number of Dentists and Dental Hygienists, but Full Effect of Federal Efforts Is Unknown

One federal effort to improve access to dental services in underserved areas is the Health Center program. To support the expansion of dental services in health centers, HRSA reported that it provided grant opportunities for health centers to expand oral health services, making 312 awards between 2002 and 2009 totaling $56.4 million. The number of patients, including children, that HRSA reported as receiving dental services in health centers, the number of FTE dentists, and the number of FTE dental hygienists providing those services all increased by more than one-third between calendar years 2006 and 2009 (see fig. 3).[44] In addition to dental services required of health centers, such as pediatric dental screenings and preventive dental services, HRSA reported a 40 percent increase in the number of patients receiving restorative dental services over this period.[45] Despite these increases, an official with the National Association of Community Health Centers reported continued need for additional health centers and dental providers to practice in them to meet the needs of underserved areas.[46]

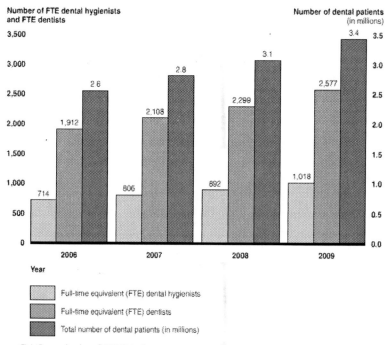

Source: GAO analysis of HRSA data.

Note: This figure presents information HRSA reported on the number of FTE dental hygienists and dentists practicing in health centers for each calendar year and the total number of dental patients. HRSA reported the exact number of patients receiving dental services as follows: 2,577,003 in 2006, 2,808,418 in 2007, 3,071,085 in 2008, and 3,438,340 in 2009.

Figure 3. Number of Dental Hygienists, Dentists, and Dental Patients at Health Centers, Calendar Years 2006 through 2009.

Another HHS program reporting an increase in the number of dentists and dental hygienists practicing in underserved areas is the NHSC. HRSA reported that 611 dentists and 70 dental hygienists were practicing in HPSAs through the NHSC scholarship and loan repayment programs at the end of fiscal year 2009.[47]

This was at least 30 percent higher than the number of NHSC dentists and dental hygienists HRSA reported as practicing in HPSAs through the program at the end of the three preceding fiscal years (see fig. 4). Despite this increase, the NHSC reported vacancies for 673 dentists and 192 dental hygienists to practice in dental HPSAs in August 2010.

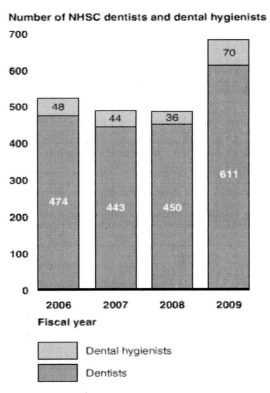

Number of NHSC dentists and dental hygienists

Source: GAO analysis of HRSA data.

Notes: This figure presents information HRSA reported on the number of dentists and dental hygienists practicing in shortage areas through the NHSC as of the end of each fiscal year.

Figure 4. Number of NHSC Dentists and Dental Hygienists Practicing in Shortage Areas, Fiscal Years 2006 through 2009.

In 2009, the Recovery Act provided appropriations for both the Health Center and NHSC programs, funding activities to improve access to services, including dental services for children, in underserved areas.

For example, according to HRSA, Recovery Act funds were used to support NHSC loan repayment awards for 96 of the dentists and 20 of the dental hygienists practicing in HPSAs through the NHSC at the end of fiscal year 2009[48] as well as an additional 382 dentists and 105 dental hygienists who received NHSC loan repayment awards in fiscal year 2010. HHS also indicated that it used funds made available through the Recovery Act to award more than 1,100 grants totaling approximately $338 million to health centers to support efforts to increase the number of patients served.[49]

Another recent statute—PPACA—authorized and in some cases appropriated funding for both the Health Center and NHSC programs. For example, in August 2010, HHS announced the availability of $250 million in grants—from funds made available in PPACA—for new full-time service delivery sites that provide comprehensive primary and preventive health care services, including pediatric dental screenings and preventive dental services, for underserved and vulnerable populations under the Health Center program. The full effect of PPACA funding on children's access to dental services in underserved areas, however, remains to be seen. See appendix III for additional information on the funding made available to the NHSC and Health Center programs through the Recovery Act and PPACA.

HHS's Oral Health Initiative 2010 and Other HHS Programs May Improve Access to Dental Services for Children in Underserved Areas

In an effort to increase support for and expand the department's emphasis on access to oral health care, including access for underserved populations, HHS launched a departmentwide Oral Health Initiative in April 2010 to improve the nation's oral health by better coordinating federal programs. According to HHS, the initiative is intended to improve the effective delivery of services to underserved populations by creating and financing programs to emphasize oral health promotion and disease prevention, increase access to care, enhance the oral health workforce, and eliminate oral health disparities.[50] The initiative includes two new HHS efforts targeted at specific groups of children that, although too early to tell, may lead to improved access for children in underserved areas:

- HHS's Administration for Children and Families has started the Head Start Dental Homes Initiative, to establish a national network of dental homes for children in Head Start and Early Head Start. The Administration for Children and Families Office of Head Start and the American Academy of Pediatric Dentistry define a dental home as comprehensive, continuously accessible, coordinated, and family-centered oral health care delivered to children by a licensed dentist.
- HHS's Indian Health Service has started the Early Childhood Caries Initiative to promote the prevention and early intervention of dental caries (tooth decay) for young American Indian and Alaska Native children—a population that experiences dental caries at a higher rate than the general U.S. population.[51]

In addition to the NHSC and Health Center programs, HHS administers, or has authority to administer, a number of other oral health programs. Although not all of these programs are targeted specifically to children in underserved areas, they may improve their access to dental services. Examples of such programs include: (1) the School-Based Dental Sealant Program, which was authorized by PPACA to expand grants for school-based dental sealant programs to all 50 states, territories, and Indian tribes and organizations;[52] and (2) the State Oral Health Workforce Grant program which awards grants to states to address workforce issues, including those associated with dental HPSAs. See appendix IY for a list of these and other HHS programs that may improve access to dental services in underserved areas.

USE OF MID-LEVEL DENTAL PROVIDERS IS NOT WIDESPREAD IN THE UNITED STATES, AND OTHER COUNTRIES HAVE USED THEM TO IMPROVE CHILDREN'S ACCESS TO DENTAL SERVICES

Mid-level dental providers—providers who can perform intermediate restorative procedures, such as drilling and filling a tooth, under remote supervision of a licensed dentist—are not widely licensed or certified to practice in the United States. Other countries, which have used mid-level dental providers for many years, reported that these providers deliver quality care and increase children's access to dental services.

Efforts Are under Way to Use Mid-Level and Other Dental Providers to Improve Children's Access to Dental Services

Within the United States, experience with mid-level dental providers is limited to the Dental Health Aide Therapist program for Alaska Natives and the advanced dental therapy program in Minnesota.[53] Efforts are under way to increase access to dental services through the use of dental therapists, dental hygienists, physicians, and other new dental provider models.

Dental Health Aide Therapist Program for Alaska Natives

The Dental Health Aide Therapist program in Alaska, the only mid-level dental provider program with providers practicing in the United States as of July 2010, began in 2003 in response to the extensive dental health needs of Alaska Natives and high dentist vacancy rates in rural Alaska.[54] Dental health aide therapists (dental therapists) in Alaska are not licensed by the state; rather the program is authorized under the federal Community Health Aide Program for Alaska Natives. The 2-year training program is based on a long-standing dental therapy program in New Zealand. After completion of their training and preceptorship, dental therapists become certified and practice in their assigned villages under the remote consultative supervision of a dentist.[55] Services performed by dental therapists may include assessments and basic and intermediate restorative procedures. As of June 2010, 19 dental therapists were serving in rural Alaska native villages or completing their preceptorship with a supervising dentist.

Children are an important focus of the Dental Health Aide Therapist program. According to an official from the Alaska Native Tribal Health Consortium, about half of the patients seen by dental therapists under this program are children. For example, between 2006 and 2009, approximately 59 percent of encounters for one dental therapist were with children under 18 years old. Consortium officials also noted that Medicaid is a major payer for dental therapist services, indicating that dental therapists provide a substantial portion of their services to children under Medicaid.[56] Although limited research regarding the impact of this program has been completed, a 2008 study examining the quality of restorative procedures performed by dental therapists found that procedures provided by dental therapists do not differ from similar procedures performed by dentists.[57] In addition, in October 2010, a study of the Dental Health Aide Therapist program found that the five dental therapists who were included in the study performed well, operated safely, and were technically competent to perform procedures within their defined scope of practice. The study also noted that the patients of the dental therapists were generally very satisfied with the care they received from those therapists. The study assessed the quality of services and procedures provided by dental therapists using various methods including patient and oral health surveys, observations of clinical technical performance, medical chart audits, and facility evaluations.[58] See appendix V for more information on the Dental Health Aide Therapist program in Alaska.

Minnesota's Advanced Dental Therapist Program

In 2009, Minnesota authorized the certification of the advanced dental therapist and dental therapist positions to provide dental services to low-income, uninsured, and underserved patients.[59] Advanced dental therapists are licensed dental therapists who, upon completion of additional education and experience, may become certified to perform a range of preventive, and basic and intermediate restorative procedures—including drilling and filling and non-surgical extractions of permanent teeth—under the remote consultative supervision of a dentist. They may also develop patient treatment plans with authorization by a consulting dentist.[60]

Advanced dental therapy training is offered by Metropolitan State University as a master's degree program which prepares students with an existing dental hygiene license for licensure as a dental therapist and certification as an advanced dental therapist upon completion of 2,000 hours of dental therapy practice.[61] As of June 2010, certification requirements for advanced dental therapists had not yet been finalized, and there were no practicing advanced dental therapists. State officials anticipated that the first advanced dental therapists will graduate in 2011. Once licensed, advanced dental therapists are required to enter into consultative agreements—which outline any restrictions to their scope of practice—with licensed dentists to whom they will refer patients for services beyond their scope of practice.[62] Minnesota health officials anticipated that advanced dental therapists will be eligible to receive direct Medicaid and CHIP reimbursement, but payment arrangements had not been finalized as of June 2010.

Use of Dental Hygienists and Physicians in Selected States

Certain states have made efforts to increase children's access to dental services by allowing dental hygienists and primary care physicians to provide certain dental services without the on-site supervision of a dentist.

In seven of the eight states we examined—Alaska, California, Colorado, Minnesota, Mississippi, Oregon, and Washington—dental hygienists may perform certain procedures, such as fluoride application, under remote or no supervision of a dentist; in some cases specifically to increase access for underserved populations.[63] For example, dental hygienists in California, Minnesota, Mississippi, Oregon, and Washington may practice in limited settings outside the private dental office under remote or no supervision of a dentist, increasing access to dental services for underserved populations, including children. Such practices are generally limited to settings such as schools or residential facilities and, in most cases, allow hygienists to provide only preventive services upon completion of additional training or clinical experience. Dental hygienists in these states increase the available locations for individuals to access certain preventive dental procedures.

In addition, five of the eight states we studied—California, Colorado, Minnesota, Oregon, and Washington— reported that they allow direct Medicaid and in some cases CHIP reimbursement to certain dental hygienists for providing some preventive dental services. [64] See appendix VI for additional information on the scope of practice and requirements for dental therapists, dental hygienists, and dental assistants in the eight states we examined.

In addition, many states have also engaged primary care medical providers—such as physicians—in the provision of children's dental services. A survey conducted in 2009 indicated that 34 state Medicaid programs reimburse primary care medical providers for providing preventive dental procedures, such as fluoride application, and this represents an increase of nine states from a similar study conducted in 2008.[65] To track the provision of dental services by physicians and dental hygienists to children covered by Medicaid, CMS officials reported that they are in the process of revising the CMS 416 to collect information on the number of children receiving dental services—such as sealants and oral assessments—from these providers and expect states will use the revised forms in 2011.

Efforts to Train or Employ New Dental Providers

In addition to state initiatives, PPACA authorized demonstration projects to train or employ certain dental providers. In March 2010, PPACA authorized $60 million to fund 15 demonstration projects to train or to employ "alternative dental health care providers" to increase access to dental services in rural and other underserved communities.

PPACA defines alternative dental health care providers to include dental therapists, independent dental hygienists, advanced practice dental hygienists, primary care physicians, and any other health professionals that HHS determines appropriate.[66] Entities eligible to apply for the demonstration grants include colleges, public-private partnerships, federally qualified health centers, Indian Health Service facilities, state or county public health clinics, and public hospital or health systems.

Two professional organizations have also proposed new dental provider models to increase children's access to dental services:

- The American Dental Association developed the position of a community dental health coordinator as a new type of dental provider who may provide oral health education as well as some preventive services (depending on the state dental practice laws) under the supervision of a dentist in communities with little access to dental care. The association has begun a community dental health coordinator pilot training program, and as of July 2010, there were 27 students in three locations in California, Oklahoma, and Pennsylvania. The training includes a 12-month online training program through Rio Salado College and a 6-month clinical internship.[67] Officials from the American Dental Association told us they plan to train 18 additional community dental health coordinators by September 2012, and they anticipated all of these providers will serve in their home communities after the training program. The American Dental Association is currently designing an evaluation of the program to be completed in 2013, one year after the pilot training program ends in 2012.

- The American Dental Hygienists' Association developed and proposed the advanced dental hygiene practitioner as a mid-level dental provider to work independently in a variety of settings to provide preventive and certain basic and intermediate restorative services—including procedures such as drilling and filling a tooth—to underserved populations. The model is similar to the advanced dental therapist position in Minnesota and proposes a master's degree curriculum that builds upon existing dental hygiene education programs.[68]

Other Countries Have Used Mid-Level Dental Providers to Improve Access to Dental Services

Mid-level dental providers—dental therapists—have been used by many countries to improve access to preventive and restorative dental services. In particular, New Zealand, the United Kingdom, Australia, and Canada have long-standing dental therapist programs.[69] These countries have used dental therapists to staff school- and community-based dental programs aimed at improving access to dental services for children and other underserved populations, such as those in rural areas (see table 6).[70] Since the mid-1990s, three of the four countries—New Zealand, the United Kingdom, and Australia—have combined their dental therapy and dental hygiene training programs.[71]

Dental therapists in the four countries, including those trained in combined oral health therapy programs, can perform preventive and basic and intermediate restorative procedures for children and adults without the on-site supervision of a dentist in both the public and private sectors. New Zealand, Australia, and Canada also permit dental therapists to determine patient treatment plans providing they maintain a relationship with a dentist where they can refer patients for services beyond their scope of practice. See appendix VII for more information on the use of dental therapists in these countries.

Health officials from the four countries expressed no reservations about the quality of care provided by dental therapists. Although recent data on the quality of services provided by dental therapists in these countries are limited, a study published in 2009 on Australian dental therapists reported that the standard of restorative procedures performed by dental therapists was comparable to the standard expected of newly graduated dentists in that country.[72]

Health officials from New Zealand, Australia, and Canada reported that the majority of dental therapists' patients are children and available research found that dental therapists providing care in school- or community-based programs were an important part of improving dental outcomes for children.[73]

For example, a health official from New Zealand—where dental therapists provide dental services in school-based clinics—told us that nearly all children aged 5 to 12 (96 percent) were enrolled in the nation's publicly funded school-based dental program in 2009.

Table 6. Characteristics of Mid-Level Dental Providers in New Zealand, the United Kingdom, Australia, and Canada

Country (year program started) Type of mid-level dental provider[a]	Scope of practice	Supervision	Years of post secondary education[a]	Number licensed or practicing (year)
New Zealand (1921)				
Dental therapist/ Oral health therapist	• Preventive • Restorative (basic and intermediate)	Remote: consultative	3	730 (2009)
United Kingdom (1959)				
Dental therapist/ Oral health therapist	• Preventive • Restorative (basic and intermediate)	Remote: prior knowledge and consent	3	1,480 (2010)
Australia[b] (1966)				
Dental therapist/ Oral health therapist	• Preventive •Restorative (basic and intermediate)	Remote: consultative	3	1,760 (2005)
Canada (1972)				
Dental therapist	• Preventive • Restorative (basic and intermediate)	Remote: prior knowledge and consent	2	310[c] (2010)

Source: GAO analysis.

Note: In these countries, most dental therapists are paid through the government as salaried employees. However, some work in private practice and are then paid by their employers. The information in this table was obtained from interviews with health officials in the four countries, professional organizations, government reports, and published research. We did not conduct an independent review of the legal authorities for this information.

[a] Since the mid-1990s, Australia, the United Kingdom, and New Zealand have combined their dental therapy and dental hygiene programs with many offered as a bachelor's degree. The required education for the combined degree is between 2 and 3 years and graduates are trained in both scopes of practice.

[b] Until July 2010, dental therapy registration differed among Australia's states with three states allowing dental therapists to provide services to adults. Australia implemented a national registration scheme in July 2010 that will require all states to have the same scope of practice.

[c] Approximately three-quarters of dental therapists (230 of 310) in Canada practice in Saskatchewan, the only province where they are registered providers and able to work in private practice.

The program aims to see all enrolled children annually (or more frequently in high-risk cases) and the official told us that available data indicated that decay rates are reduced for these children. A New Zealand national oral health survey, planned for publication in December 2010, was expected to provide a clearer picture of children's oral health status across the population. In addition, one academic dental therapy official told us that in 2010 between 40 and 70 percent of Australian children, depending on the state, obtained dental services through publicly funded school-based dental programs primarily staffed by dental therapists. A 2008 study in Australia found that, from 1977 to 2002, the number of decayed, missing, and filled teeth declined 37 percent for primary teeth in 6-year old children and 79 percent for permanent teeth in 12-year old children enrolled in school-based programs.[74] A Canadian health official reported that dental therapists serving aboriginal children in rural provinces and territories since the 1970s have often been the only reliable source of dental care for those children, in part because dentists are difficult to retain in rural areas. In the Canadian province of Saskatchewan, research on the impact of the province's school-based dental program estimated that the program served over 80 percent of non-aboriginal children in the province from 1976 to 1980 and that lower incidence of dental caries could be demonstrated with increased exposure to the program.[75] An official from the Saskatchewan Dental Therapists Association—the dental therapy regulating authority in the province—also reported that dental therapists working in private practice in the province increase children's access to dental services because they can provide restorative services and free time for dentists to see more patients. Since 2004, Canada has piloted and expanded the use of dental therapists to provide preventive and restorative services to aboriginal children in a community-based dental program. As of May 2010, Canadian health officials were completing an evaluation of the program, which they expected to show improved dental outcomes.

CONCLUSION

In the decade that has passed since the Surgeon General described the silent epidemic of oral disease affecting children in low-income families, dental disease and access to dental services have remained a significant problem for these children—including those in Medicaid and CHIP. States report that nationwide, only 36 percent of children in Medicaid received any dental service in fiscal year 2008, far below HHS's Healthy People 2010 target of 66 percent for low-income children. States also continue to report low participation by dentists in Medicaid and CHIP. Recognizing this challenge, HHS has taken a number of steps to strengthen its dental programs, including its HHS Oral Health Initiative 2010, and recent legislation has authorized and in some cases appropriated funding specifically for programs that may help increase access to dental services in underserved areas; but results of these efforts are yet to be seen. And while states report some improvement in the provision of Medicaid dental services between 2001 and 2008, CMS has not yet collected comprehensive data on utilization of dental services for children in Medicaid managed care programs and covered by CHIP. We have reported in the past that such gaps limit CMS's oversight of the provision of dental services for children, such as its ability to identify problems with specific service delivery methods.

Providing complete and accurate information to help families with children in the Medicaid and CHIP programs find dental care is an important tool in improving access. The information that HHS is required to post on its Insure Kids Now Web site could provide a useful tool for connecting these children and their families with dentists who will treat them. However, we found problems that limit its ability to do so, such as incorrect, outdated, or incomplete information; links to state Web sites that were not working; and even a dentist taking Medicaid patients who had been excluded by HHS from participation in the program. Addressing these problems—such as providing alternative sources of information to assist users when the Web site is not functioning or taken offline for maintenance, or providing additional guidance on dentists' ability to serve children with special needs—could help make the site more useful to beneficiaries.

RECOMMENDATIONS FOR EXECUTIVE ACTION

We are making several recommendations to enhance the provision of dental care to children covered by Medicaid and CHIP.

First, to help ensure that HHS's Insure Kids Now Web site is a useful tool to help connect children covered by Medicaid and CHIP with participating dentists who will treat them, we recommend that the Secretary of HHS take the following actions:

- Establish a process to periodically verify that the dentist lists posted by states on the Insure Kids Now Web site are complete, usable, and accurate, and ensure that states and participating dentists have a common understanding of what it means for a dentist to indicate he or she can treat children with special needs.
- Provide alternate sources of information, such as HHS's toll-free 1-877- KIDS-NOW telephone number, on the Insure Kids Now Web site when a page or link from the Web site is not functioning or taken offline for maintenance.
- Require states to verify that dentists listed on the Insure Kids Now Web site have not been excluded from Medicaid and CHIP by the HHS-OIG, and periodically verify that excluded providers are not included on the lists posted by the states.

Second, to strengthen CMS oversight of Medicaid and CHIP dental services provided by dental managed care programs, we recommend that the Administrator of CMS take steps to ensure that states gather comprehensive and reliable data on the provision of Medicaid and CHIP dental services by managed care programs.

AGENCY COMMENTS

We provided a draft of this report for comment to HHS. HHS agreed with our recommendations and provided written comments, which we summarize below. The text of HHS's letter—which included comments from CMS, HRSA, and CDC—is reprinted in appendix VIII. HHS also provided technical comments, which we incorporated as appropriate.

In commenting on our recommendation that steps should be taken to improve the Insure Kids Now Web site, CMS and HRSA concurred that more attention needs to be devoted to improve the accuracy of information submitted by the states. To that end, CMS and HRSA commented that they will undertake several actions:

- To address errors on the site, CMS stated that the agency will increase the type and frequency of checks performed and work with states to ensure that they submit data that are free of the types of problems we identified. HRSA commented that it will work with CMS to develop a plan to periodically analyze a sample of data provided by states to assess its accuracy.

- To ensure that providers that HHS has excluded from Medicaid and CHIP are not listed on the site, CMS commented that it will ensure states are aware that such providers must not be included in the data, and HRSA reported that it plans to cross-check listed providers against the HHSOIG's database of excluded parties.
- CMS commented that it will ensure that there is a consistent understanding of what it means to be identified on the site as a dentist serving children with special needs.

CMS agreed with our recommendation that the agency take steps to ensure that states gather comprehensive and reliable data on the provision of Medicaid and CHIP dental services by managed care programs, noting that the agency is in the process of revising the CMS 416 to include more information about dental services provided to children in state Medicaid programs, including under managed care payment arrangements. CMS's comments do not specify whether the agency will require states to separately report utilization under managed care for children in Medicaid or CHIP, a step that we believe is necessary for effective oversight.

In addition, CDC commented that a statement in the introduction of our report regarding the prevalence of tooth decay and dental disease in children may be misleading. Although our statement accurately reflects information that we previously reported, we revised the language to clarify that the results of our analysis specifically refer to children enrolled in Medicaid.

We are sending copies of this report to the Secretary of Health and Human Services and other interested parties. In addition, the report will be available at no charge on the GAO Web site at http://www.gao.gov.

If you or your staff have any questions regarding this report, please contact me at (202) 512-7114 or iritanik@gao.gov. Contact points for our Offices of Congressional Relations and Public Affairs may be found on the last page of this report. GAO staff who made major contributions to this report are listed in appendix IX.

Katherine Iritani
Acting Director,
Health Care

APPENDIX I: SCOPE AND METHODOLOGY

To address the objectives in our review—to examine (1) the extent to which dentists participate in Medicaid and the Children's Health Insurance Program (CHIP) and federal efforts to help families find dentists to treat children in these programs, (2) what is known about access for Medicaid and CHIP children in different states and in managed care, (3) federal efforts under way to improve access to dental services by children in underserved areas, and (4) how states and other countries have used midlevel dental providers to improve children's access to dental services—we interviewed appropriate officials from the Department of Health and Human Services (HHS), academic institutions, professional associations, states, and dental and children's advocacy groups; reviewed federal and state laws and regulations; obtained, reviewed, and determined the reliability of data; and reviewed relevant literature.

Specifically, to determine the extent to which dentists participate in Medicaid and CHIP and federal efforts to help families find dentists to treat children in these programs, we:

- Analyzed state reported data on the number of dentists in a state treating Medicaid and CHIP patients, including data from the 2009 Association of State and Territorial Dental Directors (ASTDD) survey[1] and one of our prior reports.[2]
- Reviewed articles in peer-reviewed journals and reports on access to dental services by children with special health care needs.
- Examined states' dentist listings on HHS's Insure Kids Now Web site, including whether listings were complete, usable, and accurate:

Completeness: To examine the completeness of the information on the Web site, we conducted two reviews—in November 2009 and in April 2010—to determine whether information CMS guidance had identified as required elements were present. We examined each state's listing of dentists to determine if certain elements listed as required in the Centers for Medicare & Medicaid Services' (CMS) June 2009 guidance were present for all dentists in all Medicaid and CHIP programs operated by the state (states can have multiple dental plans within Medicaid and CHIP) and recorded instances in which data were missing or incomplete for all or some dentists. Specifically, we examined each state's listing for the presence of dentists' names, addresses, phone numbers, and specialties; whether they accepted new

Medicaid or CHIP patients; and whether they could accommodate children with special needs.[3]

Usability: In May 2010, we conducted a review of the information available on the Insure Kids Now Web site for each of the 50 states and the District of Columbia. The purpose of this review was to determine whether families seeking a dentist to treat a child covered by Medicaid or CHIP could reasonably complete the task and, if not, what types of errors prevented the site from being usable, such as whether hyperlinks functioned as expected and linked pages contained appropriate information. We tested the drop-down menus on the Web site for the Medicaid and CHIP programs in each state, conducted a general search of dentists for each program, and searched for dentists in each state's capital city and in the District of Columbia.

Accuracy: To check the accuracy of information on dentists posted on the Insure Kids Now Web site, we selected a nongeneralizable sample of dentists listed on the Web site for four states (California, Georgia, Illinois, and Vermont) that provided variation in geography, managed care penetration for Medicaid (as reported by the American Dental Association), and number of children covered by Medicaid. We selected 25 urban dentists and 15 rural dentists listed on the Insure Kids Now Web site in each state. For urban dentists, we identified the urban county with the most children in poverty, the largest city in that county, and then the zip code within that city with the most children in poverty. We then searched for general dentists nearest to the selected zip code.[4] For rural dentists, we selected general dentists in the rural counties with the most children in poverty, excluding rural counties adjacent to major metropolitan areas.

We limited our searches to dentists listed as accepting new Medicaid and CHIP patients. We used U.S. Census data and an urban/rural classification system developed by the U.S. Department of Agriculture (called Rural-Urban Continuum Codes) to identify the areas from which we selected dentists. In May 2010, we called the telephone number listed for the selected dentists and asked the person scheduling appointments if the listed dentist currently accepted new patients, including new patients enrolled in the state's Medicaid and CHIP programs. We also asked whether the dentist accommodated children with special health care needs—generally, and specifically with regard to wheelchair access and ability to treat children requiring sedation. Finally, we asked if the listed address was accurate and inquired about the next available appointment time. In the course of making calls we contacted more than 40 dentists in some states because some offices had multiple dentists listed on the Web site, resulting in a total of 188 dentists included in our calls.

- Reviewed the literature, including our past reports and peer-reviewed journals, on factors that impact dentists' decisions to participate in Medicaid and states' efforts to address barriers to dentists' participation.

To examine what is known about access for children in Medicaid and CHIP in different states, including for children in managed care, we examined dental utilization data on children covered by Medicaid, including those covered under Medicaid expansion programs, reported by states to CMS through the annual CMS 416 form. For each state and nationally, we calculated utilization rates reported for any dental service, preventive dental services, and dental treatment services. We calculated utilization rates for federal fiscal year 2001, the year after our first report on oral health, and federal fiscal year 2008, the most recent year for which data were available. In addition, we compared children's utilization of any dental service to data reported by the American Dental Association on the proportion of children in each state who receive their Medicaid dental benefits through managed care.

To identify federal efforts under way to improve access to dental services by children in underserved areas we interviewed cognizant HHS officials, including those from CMS and the Health Resources and Services Administration (HRSA), and obtained written responses from agency officials to specific questions about relevant programs. We obtained data on health center and National Health Service Corps (NHSC) dental provider numbers and HHS program funding levels from HHS officials and documents such as annual HRSA budget justifications. We also reviewed provisions in the Recovery Act and the Patient Protection and Affordable Care Act (PPACA) legislation and interviewed HHS officials to discuss legislative changes and funding authorized and in some cases appropriated for programs that promote dental services in underserved areas.

To determine how states and other countries have used mid-level dental providers to improve dental access for children, we examined laws, regulations, and practices in eight states and interviewed or obtained written responses from relevant officials in those eight states and four countries. To select those eight states for review, we used a standard set of questions posed to relevant officials from academic institutions, professional associations, and advocacy groups regarding states' dental practice laws, including practice of mid-level dental providers. Using the standard set of questions, we obtained responses on those states considered "expansive" and those considered "restrictive" in their laws governing the practice of dental providers. We assessed the responses and, to demonstrate the variation in state laws, selected eight states—Alabama, Alaska, California, Colorado, Minnesota, Mississippi, Oregon, and Washington. To obtain information on the selected states' use of dental providers other than dentists, we conducted interviews and obtained information from Medicaid and CHIP officials and dental boards in the selected states. Our interviews with officials revealed that there is no commonly recognized definition of mid-level dental providers, therefore we defined mid-level dental providers as providers who may perform intermediate restorative procedures, such as drilling and filling a tooth, under the remote supervision of a dentist. In addition, we defined scope of practice for the purposes of this report based on interviews and review of literature and state laws. To gather information on the only practicing midlevel dental providers in the United States, we conducted a site visit to Alaska. We interviewed state and tribal officials on the Alaska Dental Health Aide Therapist program administered by the Alaska Native Tribal Health Consortium and visited two clinics where dental therapists were training and practicing. To identify efforts related to new dental provider models, we reviewed policies and proposals by professional associations and interviewed officials from academic institutions, professional associations, HHS, and our selected states. To select countries for further review, we identified four countries that use mid-level providers, specifically dental therapists, and are comparable to the United States (identified as developed countries by the CIA World Factbook[5] and with a similar percentage of children living in households with incomes below 50 percent of their country's median income). The four countries examined were Australia, Canada, New Zealand, and the United Kingdom. To obtain information on the selected countries' use of mid-level dental providers, we conducted a literature review and interviewed oral health experts and government health officials in each country.[6]

To verify the reliability of the data we used for all four objectives, including HRSA's health center data, ASTDD survey data, the American Dental Association's Medicaid managed care data, U.S. Census data, the U.S. Department of Agriculture's Rural-Urban Continuum Codes, the CMS 416 annual reports, and Alaska Dental Health Aide Therapist encounter data, we interviewed knowledgeable officials, reviewed relevant documentation, and compared the results of our analysis to published data, as appropriate. We determined that the data were sufficiently reliable for the purposes of our engagement.

We conducted this performance audit from August 2009 through November 2010 in accordance with generally accepted government auditing standards. Those standards require that we plan and perform the audit to obtain sufficient, appropriate evidence to provide a reasonable basis for our findings and conclusions based on our audit objectives. We believe that the evidence obtained provides a reasonable basis for our findings and conclusions based on our audit objectives.

APPENDIX II: MEDICAID DENTAL UTILIZATION RATES FOR FISCAL YEAR 2008

States report annually to the Centers for Medicare & Medicaid Services (CMS) on the provision of certain covered services, including dental services. Specifically, services covered under Medicaid's Early and Periodic Screening, Diagnostic, and Treatment (EPSDT) benefit are reported by states on an annual participation report, CMS 416. It captures data on the number of children who received any dental service, preventive dental service, or dental treatment service each year. We used this information to calculate state and national dental utilization rates— that is, the percentage of children eligible for EPSDT that received services in a given year (see table 7).

Table 7. Utilization of Any Dental Service, Preventive Dental Service, and Dental Treatment Service by Children in Medicaid, Ranked in Order, Fiscal Year 2008

State	Any dental service utilization	State	Preventive dental services utilization	State	Dental treatment services utilization
Idaho	56.1%	Vermont	49.9%	New Mexico	42.1%
Vermont	51.1%	Idaho	46.0%	West Virginia	41.5%
Texas	48.5%	Rhode Island	43.1%	Idaho	30.4%
New Hampshire	46.6%	New Hampshire	42.5%	Arkansas	29.9%
Nebraska	45.9%	South Carolina	42.4%	Hawaii	26.1%
Rhode Island	45.8%	Nebraska	41.6%	Massachusetts	25.1%
Iowa	45.8%	Texas	41.6%	Maine	25.1%
South Carolina	45.0%	Washington	41.4%	Texas	25.0%
Washington	45.0%	Massachusetts	40.3%	South Carolina	22.1%
Massachusetts	44.0%	North Carolina	39.9%	Nebraska	21.8%
North Carolina	43.8%	Iowa	39.4%	Vermont	21.5%
New Mexico	42.9%	Georgia	38.5%	Kentucky	21.2%
Hawaii	42.1%	Alabama	38.4%	New Hampshire	21.1%
West Virginia	41.7%	New Mexico	38.2%	Rhode Island	20.7%

Table 7. (Continued).

Georgia	41.7%	Indiana	37.1%	Virginia	20.5%
Alabama	41.6%	Hawaii	36.9%	Arizona	20.4%
Indiana	40.8%	Oklahoma	36.5%	Washington	20.4%
Oklahoma	39.2%	West Virginia	36.0%	Alaska	20.2%
Kansas	38.9%	Kansas	35.9%	Indiana	20.0%
Arizona	38.8%	Illinois	35.4%	Georgia	19.6%
Colorado	38.5%	Virginia	35.2%	North Carolina	19.2%
Mississippi	38.5%	South Dakota	34.6%	Colorado	19.1%
Virginia	38.4%	Utah	34.1%	Tennessee	19.0%
South Dakota	38.4%	Maine	33.9%	Iowa	19.0%
Illinois	38.4%	Tennessee	33.7%	Wyoming	18.9%
Kentucky	38.1%	Colorado	33.5%	Oklahoma	18.4%
Alaska	38.0%	Arizona	33.5%	New Jersey	18.0%
Tennessee	37.6%	Minnesota	32.7%	Kansas	17.9%
Maryland	37.2%	Wyoming	32.0%	Utah	17.7%
Connecticut	36.7%	Ohio	31.7%	Alabama	17.7%
Minnesota	36.7%	Mississippi	31.7%	Louisiana	17.2%
Wyoming	36.5%	Kentucky	31.6%	Minnesota	17.0%
Ohio	36.4%	Michigan	31.6%	Mississippi	16.6%
Maine	36.2%	Maryland	31.6%	Maryland	16.4%
Utah	35.0%	Arkansas	31.4%	Ohio	16.1%
Dist.Columbia	34.0%	Alaska	31.4%	Delaware	16.1%
Arkansas	33.6%	Connecticut	30.3%	California	16.0%
Delaware	33.4%	Delaware	30.1%	Oregon	15.8%
New Jersey	32.9%	District of	29.0%	Connecticut	15.4%
Oregon	32.8%	Louisiana	28.0%	New York	15.1%
Louisiana	32.5%	New Jersey	27.8%	South Dakota	14.8%
Michigan	32.4%	New York	27.6%	Illinois	14.7%
New York	32.1%	Oregon	27.6%	Michigan	13.6%
California	30.2%	Nevada	25.0%	District of	13.6%
Nevada	29.8%	California	24.5%	Montana	13.3%
North Dakota	29.1%	North Dakota	23.8%	Missouri	13.3%
Pennsylvania	26.9%	Pennsylvania	22.3%	Pennsylvania	12.9%
Montana	25.6%	Montana	22.1%	Nevada	11.7%
Missouri	24.7%	Missouri	21.9%	North Dakota	11.7%
Wisconsin	24.1%	Wisconsin	21.0%	Wisconsin	10.4%
Florida	20.9%	Florida	13.8%	Florida	7.8%
Nationwide	36.2%	Nationwide	31.5%	Nationwide	18.0%

Source: CMS Form 416 data for fiscal year 2008.

Note: This table represents dental utilization rates calculated from data reported by states in their fiscal year 2008 CMS 416 reports (the most recent available at the time of our review) on the number of EPSDT-eligible Medicaid-enrolled children who received any dental service during the fiscal year. Children enrolled in CHIP programs that are expansions of the states' Medicaid programs are entitled to the Medicaid EPSDT benefit package and are included in the states' CMS 416 reports, but are not identified separately as CHIP enrollees.

APPENDIX III: NHSC AND HEALTH CENTER FUNDING IN THE RECOVERY ACT, PPACA, AND FISCAL YEAR 2010 APPROPRIATION

The Recovery Act appropriated $500 million to address health professions workforce shortages through means such as scholarships and loan repayment awards, of which the Conference Committee directed $300 million be provided to NHSC for recruitment and field activities.[1] HRSA plans to use these funds in fiscal years 2009 through 2011.[2] For the Health Center program, the Recovery Act appropriated $2 billion for grants to benefit health centers— $500 million for grants to support the delivery of patient services and $1.5 billion for grants to support and improve health center infrastructure. According to HRSA, as of December 31, 2009, Recovery Act funds for health centers had provided support to over 550 full-time equivalent dental positions, including dentists, dental hygienists, and dental assistants, as well as dental aides, and dental technicians. HRSA reported that these positions have led to more than 575,000 dental visits to over 264,000 patients, including children, in underserved areas.

PPACA authorized and appropriated a total of $1.5 billion for NHSC for fiscal years 2011 through 2015. According to HRSA, this funding will increase the number of dentists and dental hygienists participating in NHSC. However, the agency reported that the exact number of scholarship and loan repayment awards made using these funds will depend on the number of qualified applications the program receives.[3] Additionally, PPACA authorized and appropriated $9.5 billion for health centers through the Community Health Center Fund established by the Act as well as $1.5 billion for construction and renovation of community health centers for fiscal years 2011 through 2015.[4]

Funds specifically provided for these programs in the Recovery Act and PPACA are in addition to the funds that may be specifically or generally available for the NHSC and Health Center programs through HHS's annual appropriations (see table 8).

Table 8. Funding for National Health Service Corps and Health Center Programs Under the Recovery Act and PPACA, and the Fiscal Year 2010 Annual Appropriation

Legislation/Program	Funding (appropriated) (in millions)	Funding time frame (fiscal years)
Recovery Act		
National Health Service	$300[a]	2009-2011
Health Center	$2,000	2009
PPACA		
National Health Service	$1,500	2011-2015
Health Center	$11,000[b]	2011-2015
Fiscal Year 2010 Program		
National Health Service	$142[c]	2010
Health Center	$2,190[c]	2010

Source: GAO analysis.

Note: This table presents data from the American Recovery and Reinvestment Act of 2009, Pub. L. No. 111-5, 123 Stat. 115 and H.R. Rep. No. 111-16 (2009) (Conf. Rep.); the Consolidated Appropriations Act, 2010, Pub. L. No. 111-117, Division D., Title II, 123 Stat. 3034 and H. R. Rep. No. 111-220 (2009) and S. Rep. No. 111-66 (2009); the Patient Protection and Affordable Care Act, Pub. L. No. 111-148, 124 Stat. 119 (2010); and the Health Care and Education Reconciliation Act of 2010, Pub. L. No. 111-152, 124 Stat. 1029. Funding time frames represent the fiscal years during which funding detailed in the "Funding (appropriated)" column will be available for obligation. All amounts rounded to the nearest million.

[a] Based on direction provided by the Conference Committee for the Recovery Act for specific use of the Act's appropriation to the Department of Health and Human Services. H.R. Rep. No. 111-16, at 451 (2009).

[b] As amended by the Health Care and Education Reconciliation Act of 2010. Pub. L. No 111-152, § 2303, 111 Stat.1029, 1083.

[c] Based on direction provided by the House and Senate Committees on Appropriations for specific use of the 2010 HRSA appropriation. H. R. Rep. No. 111-220, at 46, 49 (2009); S. Rep. No. 111-66, at 38, 40-41 (2009) (providing direction for HRSA appropriation contained in Consolidated Appropriations Act 2010, Pub. L. No. 111-117, Division D, Title II, 123 Stat. 3034, 3239 (2009)).

APPENDIX IV: ADDITIONAL HHS PROGRAMS THAT MAY IMPROVE ACCESS TO DENTAL SERVICES IN UNDERSERVED AREAS

In addition to the NHSC and Health Center programs, HHS administers a number of programs that, while not targeted specifically to children in underserved areas, may nevertheless improve their access to dental services in underserved areas. These include programs that target the provision of oral health services to specific populations such as schoolchildren, as well as programs that support training of oral health providers or prioritize the training of dentists and dental hygienists that could serve in underserved areas (see table 9).

Table 9. HHS Programs that May Improve Access to Dental Services in Underserved Areas

Program (Authority) HHS Agency	Program Type		Description
	Supports the Provision of Dental Services	Oral Health Workforce Training and support	
Children's Hospitals Graduate Medical Education (42 U.S.C. § 256e) HRSA		√	Provides support to freestanding children's hospitals to train medical residents, including dental residents and fellows.[a]
Grants for Training in General, Pediatric, and Public Health Dentistry (42 U.S.C. § 293k-2) HRSA		√	Awards grants to schools, hospitals, and other entities that plan, develop, operate, or participate in an approved professional training program that emphasizes training in general, pediatric, and public health dentistry.[b]
Health Professionals Student Loan Program (42 U.S.C. § 292q) HRSA		√	Awards loans to financially needy health professions students, including dental students.

Table 9. (Continued).

Program (Authority) HHS Agency	Program Type		Description
	Supports the Provision of Dental Services	Oral Health Workforce Training and Support	
Loans for Disadvantaged Students (42 U.S.C. § 292t) HRSA		√	Awards loans to health professions students from disadvantaged backgrounds, including dental students.
Ryan White Community-Based Dental Partnership and Ryan White Dental Reimbursement Programsc (42 U.S.C. § 300ff-111) HRSA	√	√	Awards grants to accredited dental education programs to increase access to oral health services for people with human immune-deficiency virus (HIV) in under-served areas by: (1) increasing the number of dentists and dental hygienists with capability manage the oral health needs of HIV positive patients; and (2) defraying unreimbursed costs associated with providing oral health care to people with HIV (applicable to the Dental Reimbursement program only).
Scholarships for Disadvantaged Students (42 U.S.C. § 293a) HRSA		√	Awards scholarships to health professions students from dis-advantaged backgrounds, including dental and dental hygiene students.
School-Based Dental Sealant Program (42 U.S.C. § 247b-14(c)) Centers for Disease Control and Prevention	√		Expands grants for school-based dental sealant programs to provide dental sealants to target populations of children.[d]
School-Based Health Centers (42 U.S.C. §§ 280h-4, 280h-5) HRSA	√		Authorizes HHS to award grants for the establishment of or for the operation of school-based health centers. Requires or authorizes HHS to give preference to applicants that serve a large population of Medicaid and CHIP children or that serve communities with high numbers of children and adolescents who are uninsured, underinsured, or enrolled in public health insurance programs[e]

State Oral Health Workforce Grants (42 U.S.C. § 256g) HRSA	√	√	Awards grants to states to address primarily workforce issues associated with dental HPSAs.[f]

Source: GAO analysis of statutes and HHS information, including grant guidance, summary information from HRSA and CDC Web sites, and information provided by agency officials.

Note: This table presents selected HHS programs that may improve access to dental services in underserved areas. While not targeted specifically to children in underserved areas, these programs may improve their access through support of the provision of dental services to specific populations or through support for oral health workforce training.

[a] HRSA reports that, in fiscal year 2009, 56 hospitals were funded through the Children's Hospitals Graduate Medical Education payment program. According to HRSA, the program enables the hospitals to support graduate medical education, enhance research, and provide care for underserved children.

[b] Statutory priority for awarding grants includes giving priority to applicants that establish formal relationships with health centers as well as applicants that have a high rate of placing residents in underserved areas.

[c] While the Ryan White Act authorizes support for institutions that may provide oral health services, these two grant programs—the Ryan White Community-Based Dental Partnership Program and the Ryan White Dental Reimbursement Program—are specifically focused on funding for dental services.

[d] As of May 2010, 16 states had grants to operate school-based or linked dental sealant programs, which generally target schools with large populations of low-income children using the percentage of children eligible for federal free and reduced-cost lunch programs. The Patient Protection and Affordable Care Act (PPACA) authorized an expansion of the program to all 50 states, territories, and Indian tribes and organizations. Dental sealants are a plastic material applied to the chewing surfaces of back teeth that have been shown to prevent tooth decay.

[e] PPACA provided for the establishment of this program and appropriated $200 million over 4 years for the establishment of school-based health centers. PPACA also authorized such sums as may be necessary for grants for program operations over 5 years, although HRSA officials reported no funding had been appropriated specifically for this purpose as of October 2010.

[f] HRSA reported that, as of October 2010, a total of 30 states had 34 grants, with California, Florida, Kansas and Ohio having two grants each. Twenty-five of these 34 active, three-year, grants were awarded in fiscal year 2009 and nine more were awarded in fiscal year 2010. All 30 states may only use the funds received under these grants for the 13 legislatively-authorized activities including, but not limited to, loan forgiveness and repayment programs for dentists who agree to practice in dental HPSAs, programs to expand or establish oral health services and facilities in dental HPSAs, and community-based prevention services—see Social Security Act 340G(b) (codified at 42 U.S.C. 256g(b)). HRSA reported that it awarded $10 million in grants in fiscal year 2009 and $17.5 million in fiscal year 2010.

APPENDIX V: DENTAL HEALTH AIDE THERAPIST PROGRAM FOR ALASKA NATIVES

Based on a 1999 oral health survey, the Indian Health Service issued a report detailing the extensive dental health needs and increasing dental vacancy rates within the Alaska Native population.[1] In order to meet the extensive dental health needs of the Alaska Native population, the Alaska Native Tribal Health Consortium (Consortium), a tribal organization managed by Alaska Native tribes through their respective regional health organizations, in collaboration with others, developed the Dental Health Aide Therapist program in 2003. This program selects individuals from rural Alaska communities to be trained and certified to practice under remote consultative supervision of dentists in the Alaska Tribal Health System. Dental health aide therapists (dental therapists) in this program in Alaska are not licensed by the state; rather the program is authorized under the federal Community Health Aide Program for Alaska Natives.

Under standards and procedures developed for this program, dental therapists must complete a 2-year training program, a 400-hour preceptorship under a dentist's supervision, and apply for certification in order to practice. Alaska's first dental therapists received their training from New Zealand's National School of Dentistry in Otago with the first dental therapists graduating in 2004. In 2007, the Consortium in partnership with the University of Washington opened the DENTEX training center and, in 2008, opened the Yuut Elitnaurivat Dental Training Clinic in partnership with the Yuut Elitnaurviat—People's Learning Center. These are the first Dental Health Aide Therapist training centers in the United States. As of March 2010, there were 13 dental therapy students enrolled in the training program.

Since 2005, dental therapists have practiced throughout Alaska. As of June 2010, 19 dental therapists had completed the 2-year training program. Of those 19, 10 dental therapists were trained in New Zealand and were certified and practicing in rural Alaska. Another five completed their preceptorships and were certified to begin practice. The remaining four dental therapists were completing their preceptorships. Figure 5 shows the areas and villages where the dental therapists were practicing or were scheduled to practice upon completion of their preceptorships. According to Consortium officials, the population of the communities where dental therapists were practicing varies from under 100 to nearly 9,000 individuals.

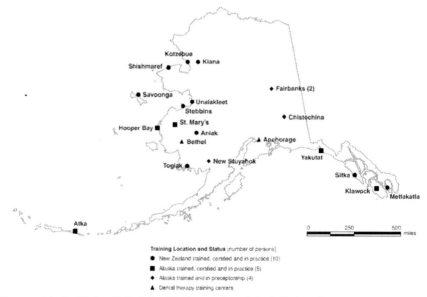

Source: Alaska Native Tribal Health Consortium; MapInfo (map).

Figure 5. Dental Therapist Training Locations and Certification Status in Alaska, June 2010.

In general, dental therapists are based in a sub-regional clinic in an Alaska Native village and travel to surrounding villages to provide services.[2] For example, one dental therapist who has been practicing at a sub-regional clinic since 2006 estimated that he travels approximately two weeks per month to the surrounding villages to provide dental services. Travel for the dental therapists, particularly in the winter, is a challenge as there are limited roads to and from the villages and in many cases air travel is the only possible mode of transport. When traveling, dental therapists often bring their own supplies into the villages and in some cases have to pack a portable dental chair.

Dental therapists treat patients primarily in rural Alaska Native communities. Although these patients are typically Alaska Native or American Indian, services may be provided to other patients, for example when the program has capacity to provide the services to others without denying or diminishing care to Alaska Native or American Indian beneficiaries or there are limited health care resources in the area. Consortium officials stated that all the tribal organizations for regions employing dental therapists generally make services available to non-Native patients, except in larger communities, such as Anchorage, Fairbanks, Juneau, and Sitka.

According to Consortium officials, dental therapists often have an agreement with the schools in their communities to allow for students to receive services during school hours. Dental therapists are trained to focus on expectant mothers and pre-school and school-aged children. Consortium officials estimate that about half of patients treated by dental therapists are children. For example, encounter data for 2006 through 2009 for two practicing dental therapists suggest that, on average, 64 percent and 59 percent of their encounters were children, respectively.[3]

APPENDIX VI: TYPES OF DENTAL PROVIDERS, EXCLUDING DENTISTS, IN EIGHT SELECTED STATES

In the states we examined—Alabama, Alaska, California, Colorado, Minnesota, Mississippi, Oregon, and Washington—a variety of dental providers other than dentists, such as dental therapists and hygienists, may provide certain services with varying degrees of supervision. Supervision of other dental providers by a dentist may take many forms. For the purposes of this report, we categorized dental supervision as: (1) the dentist must be on-site during the procedure; (2) the dentist may be off-site (remote) but must have prior knowledge of and consent to the procedures, in some cases through a treatment plan; (3) the dentist may be off-site (remote) but maintain a consultative role, for example through a signed collaborative agreement; or (4) the dentist provides no supervision (none). In addition, within each state, there is a basic level of required education and experience for each category of provider, which may increase depending on the scope of practice authorized. For example, dental hygienists in Alaska may perform preventive and basic restorative procedures under a collaborative agreement if—in addition to graduating from dental hygiene school—they have completed 4,000 hours of clinical experience. All required education and experience is listed for each type of provider.

In the eight states we examined scope of practice, required supervision, education and experience, and reimbursement varied by state. Tables 10 through 17 present information on dental providers—other than dentists—authorized to practice in those eight states.

Table 10. Selected Types of Dental Providers in Alabama, June 2010

Type of dental provider	Scope of practice[a]	Supervision required	Required education and experience	Licensed or certified	Direct Medicaid/CHIP reimbursement
Dental hygienist	• Preventive • Basic restorative	On-site	• Approved dental hygiene school, college or state program	Yes	No
Dental assistant	• Supportive • Preventive • Basic restorative	On-site	• None	No	No

Source: GAO analysis of information from state dental practice acts, state dental boards, and state officials.

[a] Each scope of practice category contains a variety of specified procedures. A provider may not be authorized to perform all procedures in a particular category.

Table 11. Selected Types of Dental Providers in Alaska, June 2010

Type of dental provider	Scope of practice[a]	Supervision required	Required education and experience	Licensed or certified	Direct Medicaid/CHIP reimbursement
Dental health aide therapist for Alaska Natives[b]	• Preventive • Basic restorative • Intermediate restorative	Remote: consultative	• Two years post-secondary training program[c] • Specified clinical experience	Yes[d]	Yes
Dental hygienist	• Preventive • Basic restorative	Remote: consultative	• Dental hygiene program	Yes	No
	• Preventive • Basic restorative	Remote: prior knowledge and consent	• Specified clinical experience • Dental hygiene program	Yes	No
	• Preventive • Basic restorative • Intermediate restorative[e]	On-site	• Dental hygiene program • Specific instructional program	Yes	No

Table 11. (Continued).

Type of dental provider	Scope of practice[a]	Supervision required	Required education and experience	Licensed or certified	Direct Medicaid/CHIP reimbursement
Dental assistant	• Supportive Preventive • Basic restorative • Intermediate restorative[e]	On-site	• Specific instructional program	Yes	No
	• Supportive • Preventive[f]	On-site	• None	No	No

Source: GAO analysis of information from state dental practice acts, state dental boards, and state and tribal officials.

[a] Each scope of practice category contains a variety of specified procedures. A provider may not be authorized to perform all procedures in a particular category.

[b] The Dental Health Aide Therapist program is authorized under the federal Community Health Aide Program for Alaska Natives, not the state.

[c] Dental health aide therapists are recruited from Alaska communities.

[d] Dental health aide therapists are not licensed by the state; rather they are certified by the Alaska Native Tribal Health Consortium as part of the federal Community Health Aide Program for Alaska Natives.

[e] State regulations establishing specific restorative function requirements have not yet been established.

[f] Dental assistants may perform certain preventive procedures such as coronal polishing, with appropriate certification which would require the completion of a specific instructional program. They may perform other preventive procedures such as the application of sealants with no additional training.

Table 12. Selected Types of Dental Providers in California, June 2010

Type of dental provider	Scope of practice[a]	Supervision required	Required education and experience	Licensed or certified	Direct Medicaid/CHIP reimbursement
Dental hygienist	• Preventive [limited settings][b]	Remote: consultative	• Dental hygiene program/bachelor's degree • Specified clinical experience • Approved post-licensure training	Yes[c]	Yes[d]
	• Preventive • Basic restorative	On-site	• Dental hygiene program • Approved post-licensure training	Yes[e]	No
	• Preventive • Basic restorative		• Dental hygiene program • Specific instructional program	Yesf	
Type of dental provider	Scope of practice[a]	Supervision required	Required education and experience	Licensed or certified	Direct Medicaid/CHIP reimbursement
	• Preventive	Remote: prior knowledge and consent	• Dental hygiene program	Yes[f]	No

Table 12. (Continued).

Type of dental provider	Scope of practice[a]	Supervision required	Required education and experience	Licensed or certified	Direct Medicaid/CHIP reimbursement
Dental assistant	• Supportive • Preventive • Basic restorative	On-site	• Specific instructional program • Specified clinical experience • Specified post-licensure training	Yes	No
	• Supportive • Preventive	On-site	• Specific instructional program • Specified clinical experience	Yes	No
	• Supportive • Preventive	On-site	• None	No	No

Source: GAO analysis of information from state dental practice acts, state dental boards, and state officials.

[a] Each scope of practice category contains a variety of specified procedures. A provider may not be authorized to perform all procedures in a particular category.

[b] Certain dental hygienists may provide preventive services in specific settings, such as schools, homebound residences, and residential facilities under remote consultative dentist's supervision.

[c] Dental hygienists with this type of license are known as registered dental hygienists in alternative practice.

[d] California CHIP does not contract with providers directly; the managed care plans reimburse providers. California Medicaid does reimburse certain licensed dental hygienists.

[e] Dental hygienists with this type of license are known as registered dental hygienists in extended function.

[f] Dental hygienists with this type of license are known as registered dental hygienists.

Table 13. Selected Types of Dental Providers in Colorado, June 2010

Type of dental provider[a]	Scope of practice[a]	Supervision required	Required education and experience	Licensed or certified	Direct Medicaid/CHIP reimbursement
Dental hygienist	• Preventive	None	• Dental hygiene program	Yes[b]	Yes[c]
	• Preventive • Basic restorative	Remote: prior knowledge and consent	• Dental hygiene program	Yes	Yes[c]
Dental assistant	• Supportive • Preventive • Basic restorative	On-site[d]	• None	No	No

Source: GAO analysis of information from state dental practice acts, state dental boards, and state officials.

[a] Each scope of practice category contains a variety of specified procedures. A provider may not be authorized to perform all procedures in a particular category.

[b] Unsupervised dental hygienists are known as independent dental hygienists and operate under the same license as other hygienists in the state.

[c] Dental hygienists may be paid directly for dental services under Medicaid. Under CHIP, only dental hygienists enrolled in a specific state program are paid directly for their services.

[d] Performance of some procedures may require prior knowledge and consent of a dentist, but not on-site supervision.

Table 14. Selected Types of Dental Providers in Minnesota, June 2010

Type of dental provider[a]	Scope of practice[a]	Supervision required	Required education and experience	Licensed or certified	Direct Medicaid/CHIP reimbursement
Advanced dental therapist [limited setting][b]	• Preventive • Basic restorative • Intermediate restorative	Remote: prior knowledge and consent[c]	• Master's level program • Specified clinical experience	Yes[d]	Not yet determined
Dental therapist [limited setting][b]	• Preventive • Basic restorative • Intermediate restorative	On-site[e]	• Bachelor's or Master's level program	Yes[d]	Not yet determined
Dental hygienist	• Preventive • Basic restorative [limited setting]	Remote: consultative[f]	• Dental hygiene program • Specified clinical experience	Yes	Yes[f]
	• Preventive • Basic restorative	On-site[g]	• Dental hygiene program	Yes	No

Type of dental provider	Scope of practice[a]	Supervision required	Required education and experience	Licensed or certified	Direct Medicaid/CHIP reimbursement
Dental assistant	• Supportive • Preventive • Basic restorative	On-site[h]	• Specific instructional program	Yes	No
	• Supportive	On-site	• None	No	No

Source: GAO analysis of information from state dental practice acts, state dental boards, and state officials.

[a] Each scope of practice category contains a variety of specified procedures. A provider may not be authorized to perform all procedures in a particular category.

[b] Advanced dental therapists and dental therapists are limited to practicing in settings that serve low-income, uninsured, and underserved populations or in a dental health professional shortage area.

[c] Pursuant to a collaborative agreement with a dentist, advanced dental therapists may perform all the procedures of a dental therapist—including restorative drilling and filling—under remote supervision of a dentist, as well as develop treatment plans and nonsurgical extractions of permanent teeth under remote supervision.

[d] Licensure for dental therapists and advanced dental therapists is the same. Advanced dental therapists require special certification which includes additional education, but specific requirements had not been finalized as of June 2010. As of June 2010, students were enrolled in advanced dental therapy and dental therapy training programs, but none were yet practicing.

[e] Pursuant to a collaborative agreement with a dentist, dental therapists may perform some preventive and basic restorative procedures off-site with prior knowledge and consent of a dentist, other procedures require on-site supervision.

[f] Pursuant to a collaborative agreement with a dentist, dental hygienists may be authorized to provide services in a health care facility, program, or nonprofit organization. These services may result in direct-to-provider Medicaid reimbursement.

[g] Dental hygienists may perform certain preventive and basic restorative procedures without the dentist being present in the dental office if the procedures being performed are with prior knowledge and consent of a dentist; other procedures require on-site supervision.

[h] Registered dental assistants may perform certain preventive and basic restorative procedures without the dentist being present in the dental office if the procedures being performed are with prior knowledge and consent of a dentist; other procedures require on-site supervision.

Table 15. Selected Types of Dental Providers in Mississippi, June 2010

Type of dental provider	Scope of practice[a]	Supervision required	Required education and experience	Licensed or certified	Direct Medicaid/CHIP reimbursement
Dental hygienist	Preventive	On-site[b]	Dental hygiene program	Yes	No
Dental assistant	Supportive Preventive[c]	On-site	None[c]	No	No

Source: GAO analysis of information from state dental practice acts, state dental boards, and state officials.

[a] Each scope of practice category contains a variety of specified procedures. A provider may not be authorized to perform all procedures in a particular category.

[b] Dental hygienists may provide preventive services outside a dental office under remote supervision through a consultative arrangement with a dentist when employed by the State Board of Health or public school boards. In addition, dental hygienists employed by the State Board of Health may apply fluoride in this context.

[c] Dental assistants must acquire a permit through the state board of dental examiners in order to take radiographs.

Table 16. Selected Types of Dental Providers in Oregon, June 2010

Type of dental provider[a]	Scope of practice[a]	Supervision required	Required education and experience	Licensed or certified	Direct Medicaid/CHIP reimbursement
Dental hygienist	• Preventive [limited setting][b]	None	• Dental hygiene program • Specified clinical experience and coursework or approved course of study including clinical experience	Yes	Yes
	• Preventive • Basic restorative	Remote: prior knowledge and consent	• Dental hygiene program • Specific instructional program	Yes	No
	• Preventive • Basic restorative	On-site	• Dental hygiene program • Specific instructional program	Yes	No
	• Preventive	Remote: prior knowledge and consent	Dental hygiene program	Yes	No
Dental assistant	• Supportive • Preventive • Basic restorative	On-site[c]	• Specific instructional programs[d]	Yes	No
	• Supportive	On-site	• None	No	No

Source: GAO analysis of information from state dental practice acts, state dental boards, and state officials.

[a] Each scope of practice category contains a variety of specified procedures. A provider may not be authorized to perform all procedures in a particular category.

[b] Dental hygienists can obtain permits to provide preventive services, including fluoride application, in limited settings such as schools and nursing homes without the supervision of a dentist. These services may result in direct-to-provider Medicaid reimbursement.

[c] Dental assistants may perform certain basic restorative procedures without the dentist being present in the dental office if the procedures being performed are with prior knowledge and consent of a dentist.

[d] Dental assistants in Oregon can obtain certification to perform various preventive and restorative services upon completion of specific instructional programs.

Table 17. Selected Types of Dental Providers in Washington, June 2010

Type of dental provider	Scope of practice[a]	Supervision required	Required education and experience[b]	Licensed or certified	Direct Medicaid/CHIP reimbursement
Dental hygienist	• Preventive [limited setting][c]	None	• Dental hygiene program • Specific instructional program	Yes	Yes
	• Preventive [limited setting]d	Remote: consultative	• Dental hygiene program • Specified clinical experience	Yes	No
	• Preventive	Remote: prior knowledge and consent	• Dental hygiene program	Yes	No
	• Preventive • Basic restorative • Intermediate restorativee	On-site	• Dental hygiene program	Yes	No
Dental assistant	• Supportive • Preventive [limited setting]f	Remote: prior knowledge and consent	• Program-specific instructional program • Specified clinical experience	Yesg	No

Table 17. (Continued).

Type of dental provider	Scope of practice[a]	Supervision required	Required education and experience[b]	Licensed or certified	Direct Medicaid/CHIP reimbursement
	• Supportive • Preventive • Basic restorative	On-site[h]	• Specific instructional program or comparable credential	Yes[g]	No
	• Supportive • Preventive • Basic restorative	On-site	• None	Yes[g]	No

Source: GAO analysis of information from state dental practice acts, state dental boards, and state officials.

[a] Each scope of practice category contains a variety of specified procedures. A provider may not be authorized to perform all procedures in a particular category.

[b] All dental hygienists and dental assistants in Washington must complete AIDS education and training.

[c] Dental hygienists can become endorsed to administer sealants and fluoride varnishes and remove deposits and stains from the surfaces of teeth in school-based settings by completing a specified instructional program (hygienists licensed on or before April 19, 2001 were automatically endorsed). These services may result in direct-to-provider Medicaid reimbursement.

[d] Dental hygienists with at least two years clinical experience may provide preventive services in certain health-care facilities or senior centers under remote dentist's supervision. A consultative agreement with dentist is required to provide services in senior centers.

[e] Dental hygienists may place a restoration (filling) in a cavity prepared by a dentist.

[f] Dental assistants can become endorsed to administer sealants and fluoride varnishes in school-based settings by completing a program-specific training program and 200 hours of clinical experience (assistants employed by a licensed Washington dentist on or before April 19, 2001 were not required to obtain an endorsement).

[g] All dental assistants in Washington must be registered or licensed to practice in the state. Dental assistants must meet limited requirements to become registered. Dental assistants must meet additional educational requirements to become licensed or endorsed to perform additional or preventive procedures under remote supervision.

[h] Licensed dental assistants may perform certain preventive procedures without a dentist being present and with prior knowledge and consent of a dentist.

APPENDIX VII: SUMMARY OF FOUR SELECTED COUNTRIES' USE OF DENTAL THERAPISTS

Dental therapists practice in many countries around the world.[1] In particular, New Zealand, the United Kingdom, Australia, and Canada have long-standing dental therapy training programs originally aimed at improving access to dental services for children and other underserved populations. Below are brief descriptions of the dental therapist programs in these four countries.[2]

New Zealand

New Zealand began training dental therapists in 1921 to provide dental care to children through school-based clinics—known as the school dental service—in response to high rates of dental decay and a shortage of dentists.[3] Since 2006, dental therapy and dental hygiene training have been combined into a single 3-year bachelor's degree granting program offered through two universities.[4] Graduates of the combined programs can register as both a dental therapist and a dental hygienist.[5] Registered dental therapists can work throughout the country to determine treatment plans and provide preventive and basic and intermediate restorative services—including procedures such as drilling and filling a tooth—for children and, in some cases, adults, under remote consultative supervision of a dentist.[6] Dental therapists in New Zealand maintain a consultative relationship with a dentist and refer patients to a dentist for services beyond their scope of practice. Although dental therapists have been able to work in private practice since 2004, according to a 2007 study, the majority of dental therapists in the country work as salaried employees for District Health Boards to provide dental services to children through the school dental service in school- and community-based dental clinics.[7] An official from the New Zealand Ministry of Health estimated that in 2009, 96 percent of children aged five to 12 in the country were enrolled in the school dental service and therefore received dental care from dental therapists.

The United Kingdom

The United Kingdom established its first dental therapy training program in 1959 to meet a growing need for dental providers to staff school- and community-based dental programs.[8] Students were selected from across the United Kingdom and were expected to return to their home areas after training. The number of dental therapy training programs has expanded in recent years, and most are offered as 3-year combined dental therapy and dental hygiene programs.[9] Dental therapists in the United Kingdom must be registered with the General Dental Council to practice and registered dental therapists may provide preventive and basic and intermediate restorative services—including procedures such as drilling and filling a tooth—for children and adults under a treatment plan developed by a dentist.[10] Until 2002, dental therapists were restricted to salaried employment in the public sector. Since then, they have been able to work in independent practice, and since 2006, dental therapists have been permitted to own their own practice and employ other dental professionals. According to a 2007 survey of registered dental therapists; 50 percent worked in private practice, 31 percent worked in public dental services, and 10 percent worked in both.[11] Overall, 39 percent of dental therapists reported spending most of their time treating children.[12]

Australia

Dental therapy training programs began in certain Australian states in 1966 and 1967 and expanded to all states and territories to train dental therapists to provide dental services to children through school-based dental programs—known as the school dental service.[13] In 2010, there were nine dental therapy training programs in Australia, eight of which offered a combined 3-year dental therapy and dental hygiene bachelor's degree.[14] In the past, Australia's eight states and territories were responsible for dental therapy registration, but as of July 1, 2010, Australia implemented a national registration and accreditation scheme requiring standard qualification for all dental therapists and oral health therapists registering after that date. Australian health officials reported that prior to national registration, dental therapists could generally provide primary oral health care including treatment planning, preventive and basic and intermediate restorative services— including procedures such as drilling and filling teeth for children under the remote consultative supervision of a dentist. Three Australian states—the Northern Territory, Victoria, and Western Australia—also allowed dental therapists to provide services to adults according to an Australian expert. Until recently, the majority of states and territories restricted employment of dental therapists to the public sector, however according to a 2005 national survey, 78 percent of dental therapists worked in the public sector—mostly as salaried employees of school- and community-based dental programs.[15] In Western Australia, however, which has always permitted dental therapists to work in private practice, about 55 percent of dental therapists worked in the public sector in 2005.

Canada

The first Canadian dental therapy training programs were established in the Northwest Territories and Saskatchewan in 1972 to increase access to dental services for rural and aboriginal populations with a focus on children.[16] Dental therapy practice differs across Canadian provinces and territories.[17] Dental therapy training is offered as a government funded 2-year program through the National School of Dental Therapy at the First Nations University, whose charter is to train dental therapists to treat aboriginal populations. Although the National School of Dental Therapy program is not accredited, graduates either become licensed by and practice in Saskatchewan or work for the federal government or aboriginal tribes. Canadian dental therapists may provide preventive and basic and intermediate restorative services—including procedures such as drilling and filling a tooth—for children and adults under a treatment plan provided by a dentist. As of May 2010, the majority of Canadian dental therapists worked in Saskatchewan where they must be licensed by the Saskatchewan Dental Therapists Association according to an association official.[18] Most of the dental therapists in Saskatchewan work in private dental practices, although some are directly employed by the federal or provincial government or aboriginal tribes.[19] In all other Canadian provinces and territories except Ontario and Quebec, dental therapists are generally restricted to employment through the federal or territorial government or tribes to provide care to aboriginal populations living on reservations.[20]

APPENDIX VIII:

COMMENTS FROM THE
DEPARTMENT OF HEALTH AND HUMAN SERVICES

DEPARTMENT OF HEALTH & HUMAN SERVICES   OFFICE OF THE SECRETARY

Assistant Secretary for Legislation
Washington, DC 20201

NOV 4 2010

Katherine Iritani
Director, Health Care
U.S. Government Accountability Office
441 G Street N W
Washington, DC 20548

Dear Ms. Iritani:

Attached are comments on the U.S. Government Accountability Office's (GAO) correspondence entitled: "Oral Health: Efforts Underway to Improve Children's Access to Dental Services, but Sustained Attention Needed to Address Ongoing Concerns" (GAO 11-96).

The Department appreciates the opportunity to review this correspondence before its publication .

Sincerely,

Jim R. Esquea
Assistant Secretary for Legislation

Attachment

GENERAL COMMENTS OF THE DEPARTMENT OF HEALTH AND HUMAN SERVICES (HHS) ON THE GOVERNMENT ACCOUNTABILITY OFFICE'S (GAO) DRAFT REPORT ENTITLED: "ORAL HEALTH: EFFORTS UNDERWAY TO IMPROVE CHILDREN'S ACCESS TO DENTAL SERVICES, BUT SUSTAINED ATTENTION NEEDED TO ADDRESS ONGOING CONCERNS" (GAO-11-96)

The Department appreciates the opportunity to review and comment on this draft report.

CDC agrees in general with the report. However, based on data from the National Health and Nutrition Examination Survey (NHANES) and citing a previous report, the GAO "estimated that 6.5 million children had untreated tooth decay, and rates of dental disease among younger children in Medicaid had increased." This statement may be misleading in light of more recent analysis of NHANES data by CDC's National Center for Health Statistics.

This 2010 analysis reported that among poor young children (age 2-5 years) there has been no change in rates of dental disease between 1988-94 and 1999-2004. Among poor children age 6-8 years, there has been an increase in caries experience. Among children age 2-5 years, however, the actual increase in caries seems to be significant only among the non-poor boys. Regarding untreated tooth decay, only non-poor boys have shown an increase in untreated caries among all 2-8 year-old children between NHANES 1988-94 and 1999-2004. Rates of untreated tooth decay for poor children age 2-8 years has remained unchanged.

These findings and others are published in: Dye BA, Arevalo O, Vargas CM. Trends in pediatric dental caries by poverty status in the United States, 1988-1994 and 1999-2004. International Journal of Pediatric Dentistry 2010; 20: 132-143.

It should also be noted that when reporting on caries experience or "dental disease" in young children, these constructs include both treated and untreated caries. An increase in caries experience could be driven by an increase in the dental fillings/restorations component while the untreated disease component remained unchanged. An increase in the dental restoration component could indicate an increase in dental utilization, hence improvements in access to dental care, especially for low income children. Healthy People 2010 has shown an increase in utilization of preventive services among low income children age 2-19 years.

CDC appreciates the efforts that went into this report and looks forward to working with GAO on this and other reports.

The GAO issued two recommendations for executive action. CMS concurs with each recommendation with the following comments:

GAO Recommendation

The Department of Health and Human Services should take steps to improve its Insure Kids Now Web site.

CMS Response

We agree with this recommendation and that improvement undertaken by States and the Federal government, such as those identified in this report, is much needed. Under the current process, States submit the information on their participating dental providers to the IKN website through a download tool that was developed for this purpose or through another acceptable method. A contractor (working under a Health Resources and Services Administration (HRSA) contract but in collaboration with CMS) then includes the information in a database that links to the dental provider search engine. The data is subject to a screening process in which addresses are matched against public records. However, evaluating the quality of those records has not been part of the scope of the contractor's responsibilities.

The CMS will undertake the following approaches to address this concern:

> First, to address the errors found on the Web site, the Department will increase the frequency and type of quality checks performed on State-reported dental provider information, and work with States to ensure they submit data that is complete, accurate and current. Specifically, we will follow up with States identified in the GAO report to ensure that they correct existing information on the Web site. We will also continue the process of requiring States to submit data on providers directly instead of providing links to State Web sites. We will also ensure States are aware of their responsibility to not list providers who have been excluded from participation under section 1128B of the Social Security Act; explore Federal options for cross checking lists of providers with the disenrolled provider database; and create a consistent understanding of what it means to be identified as a dental provider able to serve a child with special needs.

> We will consider additional ways, including regulatory guidance, to assure better information in implementing the provisions of CHIPRA, which may include specific requirements, parameters and timeframes for public listings of eligible, enrolled providers who are providing care to Medicaid and CHIP children, including those with special needs.

GAO Recommendation

The Administrator of CMS take steps to ensure that States gather comprehensive and reliable data on the provision of Medicaid and CHIP dental services by managed care programs.

CMS Response

We agree with this recommendation. CMS is in the process of implementing major changes that will improve collection of data related to dental services for children delivered through fee-for-service or managed care payment arrangements. A revised CMS-416 form, which is CMS's primary tool for gathering data on the provision of services to children in State Medicaid programs, is in the final stages of the clearance process and will be released to States, along with written guidance, in the near future. This revised form has been expanded to include dental data elements as required by CHIPRA. The instructions for completing the CMS-416 specify that additional data reported on the form must include data for services delivered to individuals in both fee-for-service or managed care arrangements. Several provisions of CHIPRA also establish the foundation for CMS to build an infrastructure for a quality measures program in which data are collected and reported in a uniform way for children in Medicaid and CHIP. The collection of data on dental services will benefit from CMS-wide efforts underway to improve the collection and reporting of data on quality of care measures more broadly.

The CMS is also establishing a workgroup consisting of national and local stakeholders in the field of child health that will focus on improving access to the benefits required under Early and Periodic Screening, Diagnostic, and Treatment (EPSDT) and will ask the workgroup to identify, among other things, ways to obtain more reliable data on dental services provided for children in managed care plans. This workgroup will be established by early 2011.

Other CMS Activities

The CMS has also undertaken a number of efforts to improve children's access to oral health services. To accelerate our efforts to improve access to oral health services and to provide focus and visibility to our efforts, CMS announced in April 2010 at the National Oral Health conference two national oral health goals. The goals are: 1) to increase the national rate of children and adolescents enrolled in Medicaid or CHIP who receive any preventive dental service by 10 percentage points over 5 years; and 2) to increase the rate of children ages 6-9 enrolled in Medicaid or CHIP who receive a dental sealant on a permanent molar tooth by 10 percentage points over 5 years. The dental sealant goal will be phased in during the next two to three years. Data for monitoring ongoing progress on this goal will be collected through the CMS-416 report and the CHIP State Annual Reports. Data collected for Federal fiscal year 2011 will serve as baseline data for this goal.

The CMS is collaborating with States on how to achieve these goals and we have developed an oral health strategy that identifies the principal barriers to children receiving dental care as well as some recommended approaches to overcoming these barriers. Much of the strategy was developed based on information learned during State dental reviews undertaken by CMS. In 2008, CMS examined the policies and practices of 16 States that had low dental utilization rates. In 2009, CMS began reviews of eight States that had higher than average dental utilization rates or were recommended to CMS as having an innovative practice for increasing dental access. Each State review and a summary of the State reviews will be available on the CMS Web site (http://www.cms.gov/MedicaidDentalCoverage) by the end of December 2010. The results of these State reviews can help other States improve access to dental services.

To support States in improving access to dental care, CMS will provide technical assistance to States to help improve access to children's dental care and to make progress toward achieving these goals, including:

- Identifying promising practices that States have used to increase children's access to oral health care;
- Annual meetings with States and national experts to share experiences;
- Assessing progress toward the goals;
- Identifying barriers to access; and

- Support opportunities for dental providers to receive incentive payments for meaningful use of electronic health record technology.

CMS is holding two technical assistance workshops for States to discuss CMS' dental goals and strategy. The first workshop, held on October 7, 2010 in conjunction with the National Academy for State Health Policy conference in New Orleans, Louisiana, was attended by 20 officials from CHIP or Medicaid programs, including several oral health directors. The second workshop will be held on November 10, 2010 in Arlington, Virginia following the annual conference of the National Association of State Medicaid Directors. CMS will hold a meeting with external stakeholders this year to identify areas where they may wish to support our efforts in improving access to oral health services. CMS will take feedback from all of these meetings into consideration as we finalize our oral health strategy.

The CMS' goals and dental strategy support the larger HHS Oral Health Initiative 2010 and the Department's comprehensive commitment to improved oral health. CMS is coordinating with other components of the Department on this important initiative as a member of the HHS Assistant Secretary for Health's Oral Health Coordinating Committee, which brings together fourteen agencies to direct the Department's oral health activities. In order to further the collaborative efforts on oral health, CMS has entered into a Memorandum of Understanding with HRSA and the Centers for Disease Control and Prevention.

Improving access to children's dental services in Medicaid and CHIP is one of our key priorities. We appreciate the efforts that went into this report and look forward to working with the GAO on this and other issues.

HRSA has offered the following recommendations:

Under the Children's Health Insurance Program Reauthorization Act (CHIPRA), the Department of Health and Human Services (HHS) is required to post a list of oral health providers who provide services to eligible Medicaid and Children's Health Insurance Program (CHIP) children on the Insure Kids Now (IKN) web site. This list is to be updated on a quarterly basis. This initiative was a huge undertaking given that this is the first national list of any type of Medicaid and CHIP health care providers. Despite the challenges, HRSA, under an Interagency Agreement (IAA) with the Centers for Medicare and Medicaid Services (CMS), met all statutory deadlines outlined under CHIPRA and have developed an Oral Health Locator (Locator). This Locator provides information to Medicaid and CHIP enrollees on how to find dentists and other oral health providers that accept Medicaid and CHIP.

HRSA concurs with many of the findings and recommendations from the GAO report. HRSA has spent much effort in the past year working with states to improve the Locators capacity to accept and post data from states. It should be noted that while the law requires that the data on the IKN web site be updated on a quarterly basis, the system allows data to be updated on a daily basis ensuring that the most up-to-date information is available to enrollees.

HRSA has specific comments regarding the following aspects of the report found under Section titled "Information on HHS's Web Site to Help Locate Participating Dentists is Not Always Complete" beginning on page 14, first paragraph:

HRSA concurs that more attention needs to be devoted to improving the accuracy of information submitted by states. Much attention in the past year has been devoted to developing the system to allow for data submissions from states. It should be noted that data are submitted from states that utilize fee-for-service programs, and from health plans that utilize capitated or managed care programs. Given that data are received from multiple sources for one state, it is difficult to ensure the accuracy of all information.

A sampling of the data could be done on a periodic basis. It should be noted that data files are reviewed systematically to ensure that all data fields have acceptable data (e.g., a field that requires a zip code has a 5 or 9 digit numerical value). Data files that do not adhere to the business rules outlined in our technical guidance to the states are returned and not posted.

Completeness: The GAO outlines through their review, cases of missing or incomplete information including "...telephone numbers and addresses, whether dentists accepted new Medicaid or CHIP patients, and whether dentists could accommodate children with special needs." It should be noted that information concerning whether a provider is accepting new patients or accommodates children with special needs is not required under CHIPRA. This is information that CMS and HRSA thought would be important to enrollees trying to identify an oral health provider. We will continue to work with states to improve the quality of this information.

Usability: GAO noted that they found "...7 states listed multiple health plans with similar names, some containing typographical errors and some that produced different provider listings, increasing the likelihood of selecting the wrong plan and generating an incorrect list of dentists." HRSA will continue to work with the Assistant Secretary for Public Affairs (ASPA) to improve the usability of the IKN web site. It should be noted that a widget is currently being developed to make it easier for enrollees to search for an oral health provider. HRSA will also work with ASPA to ensure that all the web links are working. The system was developed bearing in mind that many enrollees may not know if they are in Medicaid or CHIP but rather may more easily associate with the health plan. HRSA has instructed states to utilize the program names identified on their Medicaid or CHIP enrollee cards.

Accuracy: HRSA will work with CMS to develop a plan for periodically analyzing a sampling of the data provided by states.

First paragraph – page 18 : In the first paragraph GAO reported concerns with providers being listed on the IKN web site that were excluded from participating in Medicaid by the HHS Office of Inspector General (OIG). HRSA will cross check the excluded parties list independently and
check with CMS on the currency of the data provided, as the system was not developed to cross check data with OIG.

End Notes

1 Children in Medicaid are generally entitled to comprehensive dental services under the program's Early and Periodic Screening, Diagnostic, and Treatment (EPSDT) benefit. And, beginning in October 2009, states were required to offer a package of dental benefits under their CHIP programs.

2 See GAO, Oral Health: Dental Disease Is a Chronic Problem Among Low-Income Populations, GAO/HEHS-00-72 (Washington, D.C.: Apr. 12, 2000), GAO, Oral Health: Factors Contributing to Low Use of Dental Services by Low-Income Populations, GAO/HEHS-00-149 (Washington, D.C.: Sept. 11, 2000), and Related GAO Products at the end of this report.

3 We used national survey data from 1999 through 2004 to estimate the number of Medicaid-enrolled children with untreated tooth decay. We also examined survey data for the 1988 through 1994 and 1999 through 2004 time periods and found that rates of dental disease had not decreased, although the data suggested the trends varied somewhat among different age groups. See GAO, Medicaid: Extent of Dental Disease in Children Has Not Decreased, and Millions Are Estimated to Have Untreated Tooth Decay, GAO-08-1121 (Washington, D.C.: Sept. 23, 2008).

4 GAO, Medicaid: State and Federal Actions Have Been Taken to Improve Children's Access to Dental Services, but Gaps Remain, GAO-09-723 (Washington, D.C.: Sept. 30, 2009).

5 Children's Health Insurance Program Reauthorization Act of 2009, Pub. L. No. 111-3, § 501(f), 123 Stat. 8, 88.

6 Pub. L. No. 111-3, § 501(f), 123 Stat. 88.

7 We selected 4 states that represented a variation in geography, use of managed care, and the number of children covered by Medicaid. Within each state we called the offices for at least 25 urban and 15 rural dentists in the areas with the largest number of children in poverty.

8 Annual EPSDT reports contain information on children who are (1) in Medicaid and received EPSDT benefits and (2) in CHIP and received EPSDT benefits because they are part of a Medicaid expansion program.

9 American Recovery and Reinvestment Act of 2009, Pub. L. No. 111-5, 123 Stat. 115; Patient Protection and Affordable Care Act, Pub. L. No. 111-148, 124 Stat. 119 (2010). References to the Patient Protection and Affordable Care Act (PPACA) in this report refer to Pub. L. No. 111-148, as amended by the Health Care and Education Reconciliation Act of 2010, Pub. L. No. 111-152, 124 Stat. 1029.

10 Our interviews with officials from HHS, states, academic institutions, professional associations, and advocacy groups found that there is no commonly-recognized definition of mid-level dental providers.

11 U.S. Department of Health and Human Services, National Institute of Dental and Craniofacial Research, National Institutes of Health, Oral Health in America: A Report of the Surgeon General (Rockville, Md.: 2000).

12 HHS established Healthy People 2010 as a statement of national health objectives designed to identify the most significant preventable threats to health and to establish national goals to reduce these threats. See http://www.healthypeople.gov/About/ (accessed Aug. 3, 2010).

13 The 30 million children represent the fiscal year 2008 unduplicated annual enrollment (the total number of children, each child counted once, who were enrolled in Medicaid at any point in federal fiscal year 2008) reported by CMS.

14 In February 2009, the Children's Health Insurance Program Reauthorization Act of 2009 renamed the State Children's Health Insurance Program (SCHIP) to the Children's Health Insurance Program (CHIP).

15 Pub. L. No. 111-3, § 501, 123 Stat. 84. CHIPRA allowed states to provide dental coverage for children in the CHIP income range who have health insurance through an employer, but who lack dental coverage.

16 Pub. L. No. 111-3, § 501(e), 123 Stat. 87.

17 Pub. L. No. 111-3, § 501(f), 123 Stat. 88. HHS's Insure Kids Now Web site was established in 1999 to help parents and guardians find state Medicaid and CHIP program eligibility information. To improve access to information on dental providers participating in Medicaid and CHIP, in February 2009, CHIPRA required HHS to post a list of participating dentists within each state on the Insure Kids Now Web site and also provide such information through its toll-free hotline (1-877-KIDS-NOW).

18 42 U.S.C. § 254b. Health centers are funded in part through grants under the Health Center program—administered by HRSA—and provide comprehensive primary care services for the medically underserved.

19 42 U.S.C. § 254d. The NHSC scholarship program provides tuition, fees, and living stipends for students in primary care, including dentistry, in exchange for at least 2 years of service. 42 U.S.C. § 254l. The NHSC loan repayment program provides up to $50,000 toward repayment of student loans for providers, including dentists and dental hygienists, in exchange for at least 2 years of service. 42 U.S.C. § 254l-1. HRSA also administers the State Loan Repayment program that provides matching grants to states to run their own loan repayment programs for health providers who agree to practice in underserved areas, which in some states includes awards for dentists and dental hygienists. 42 U.S.C. § 254 q-1.

20 42 C.F.R. pt. 5, app. B (2009); 42 U.S.C. § 254e(a)(1).

21 Of the 4,377 dental HPSAs, 790 were for geographic areas, 1,526 were for population groups, and 2,061 were facilities such as health centers that were designated as HPSAs. See http://bhpr.hrsa.gov/shortage (accessed July 14, 2010).

22 HRSA estimates the number of full-time equivalent dentists needed to remove HPSA designations by taking into account the actual level of service provided by a given dentist. For example, a HPSA needing a dentist working half-time to remove its HPSA designation would be estimated to need 0.5 FTE, although adjustments are made for a variety of factors, such as the number of dental hygienists and dental assistants.

23 To identify HPSAs of greatest shortage, HRSA scores each HPSA based on relative need. Only HPSAs meeting a certain threshold score are considered HPSAs of greatest need. This threshold may differ for scholarship recipients and loan repayment recipients in a given year.

24 The number of choices available to scholarship recipients is provided for in statute: no more than twice the number of scholarship recipients who will be available for assignment during the year. For example, if there were 25 dentists who received NHSC scholarships available for service, NHSC would provide a list of no more than 50 vacancies for them. See 42 U.S.C. § 254f-1(d)(2).

25 In the United States, dentists are licensed to practice by the states and states are generally responsible for establishing education requirements and determining scope of practice of dental providers. They can obtain additional training in a dental specialty, such as pediatric dentistry or orthodontics.

26 ASTDD's annual survey, called the Synopses of State and Territorial Dental Public Health Programs, is conducted under a cooperative agreement with HHS's Centers for Disease Control and Prevention.

27 ASTDD sent the survey to dental directors in all states and the District of Columbia. However, not all states provided responses to the questions on the number of dentists treating children in Medicaid and CHIP. For example, 39 states reported how many dentists treated children in Medicaid (including children in CHIP programs that are Medicaid expansions) and 11 reported the number of dentists who treated children in a CHIP program separate from Medicaid. See http://apps.nccd.cdc.gov/synopses/ (accessed July 21, 2010).

28 GAO/HEHS-00-149.

29 Association of State and Territorial Dental Directors, ASTDD Support for State CSHCN Oral Health Forums, Action Plans And Follow-Up Activities; Interim Evaluation Summary (March 2009).

30 Burton L. Edelstein, "Conceptual Frameworks for Understanding System Capacity in the Care of People with Special Health Care Needs," Pediatric Dentistry, Vol. 29, No. 2 (March/April 2007).

31 The study found that overall, 8.9 percent of children with special health care needs who needed any dental care were unable to obtain it. Children with Down's Syndrome had the highest proportion of unmet dental care needs at 17.4 percent, and children with asthma the lowest at 8.6 percent. C.W. Lewis, "Dental Care and Children with Special Health Care Needs: A Population-Based Perspective," Academic Pediatrics. Vol. 9, No. 6: 420-426 (2009).

32 Specifically, the study noted that the adjusted odds of unmet dental care needs for severely affected, poor/low-income children with special health care needs were 13.4 times that of unaffected, higher-income children.

33 The dentists were listed on the Insure Kids Now Web site as practicing in California, Georgia, Illinois, and Vermont. Our case study approach did not yield results that could be projected to entire states or managed care organizations.

34 One dentist reported that the wait time for a new Medicaid or CHIP child was 6 months, compared to 2 months for other new patients with private insurance. Twenty-three of the dentists we called who were otherwise treating children were not accepting any new Medicaid or CHIP patients.

35 HHS may exclude providers from receiving payment from federally funded health care programs, including Medicare and Medicaid, for incidents such as conviction for program-related fraud and patient abuse, license revocation or suspension, and default on Health Education Assistance Loans. See http://oig.hhs.gov/fraud/exclusions.asp (accessed July 20, 2010).

36 HHS-OIG officials told us that the dentist has been excluded from Medicaid in 1986 after pleading guilty to Medicaid fraud.

37 Children enrolled in CHIP programs that are expansions of the states' Medicaid programs are entitled to the Medicaid EPSDT benefit package and are included in the states CMS 416 reports, but are not identified separately as CHIP enrollees in the CMS 416.

38 We calculated and report the nationwide Medicaid dental utilization rate—that is, the percentage of total EPSDT-eligible Medicaid enrollees in the nation who received any dental service. CMS reports a national average of 37.7 percent in 2008 that is calculated by averaging the 51 state-utilization rates. We report the national utilization rate rather than the average rate because it accounts for differences in the number of enrollees in each state.

39 In prior work, we found concerns that data on the provision of Medicaid services by managed care programs reported by states on their CMS 416s were not complete or reliable. See GAO, Medicaid: Stronger Efforts Needed to Ensure Children's Access to Health Screening Services, GAO-01-749 (Washington, D.C.: July 13, 2001). According to CMS officials, states have improved the quality of data gathered and reported on their CMS 416 reports.

40 See American Dental Association's Medicaid Compendium Update http://www.ada.org /2123.aspx (accessed Feb. 12, 2010). We considered states with 75 percent or more Medicaid-enrolled children in dental managed care as predominantly dental managed care states.

41 GAO, Medicaid: Concerns Remain about Sufficiency of Data for Oversight of Children's Dental Services, GAO-07-826T (Washington, D.C.: May 2, 2007).

42 Social Security Act § 2108(a) (codified at 42 U.S.C. § 1397hh(a)).

43 Pub. L. No. 111-3, § 501(e), 123 Stat. 87.

44 In addition to dentists, health centers employed 1,018 dental hygienist FTEs and over 4,800 FTEs for dental assistants, aides, and technicians in calendar year 2009.

45 HRSA reported that 942 health center grantees offered restorative dental services—either directly, through contracts, or through formal referral arrangements—as of June 2010.

46 We previously reported that 43 percent of medically underserved areas lacked a health center as of 2007. GAO, Health Resources and Services Administration: Many Underserved Areas Lack a Health Center Site, and the Health Center Program Needs More Oversight, GAO-08-

723 (Washington, D.C.: Aug. 8, 2008). In August 2010, an official with the National Association of Community Health Centers told us that, although the number of underserved areas with a health center site increased since 2007, the change has not been significant and many underserved areas still lacked a health center to provide dental and other medical services.

47 Of the 611 dentists and 70 dental hygienists in NHSC at the end of fiscal year 2009, 112 dentists and 13 hygienists were funded through the State Loan Repayment Program.

48 These loan repayment awards made in fiscal year 2009 represent 16 percent of the 611 dentists and 29 percent of the 70 dental hygienists practicing in HPSAs through the NHSC at the end of fiscal year 2009.

49 These grants for increased demand for services from health centers were awarded to fund activities such as adding new providers, expanding hours, or expanding existing health center services.

50 See Promoting and Enhancing the Oral Health of the Public: HHS Oral Health Initiative 2010 for a description of the agency's efforts under this initiative: http://www.hrsa.gov /public health/clinical/oralhealth/hhsinitiative.pdf (accessed June 16, 2010).

51 The Early Childhood Caries Initiative activities include early oral health assessment by community partners such as Head Start, nurses, and physicians; fluoride varnish application by these community partners and dental teams; and the application of dental sealants on primary teeth for young children.

52 See Pub. L. No. 111-148, § 4102(b), 124 Stat. 551.

53 For the purposes of this report, in the United States, mid-level providers are known as dental therapists in Alaska under the Dental Health Aide Therapist program and advanced dental therapists in Minnesota.

54 Alaska Native children had rates of dental caries (cavities) that were 2.5 times the U.S. average and Alaska tribes experienced dentist vacancy rates of 25 percent.

55 Under standards of the Community Health Aide Program Certification Board, prior to certification, each dental therapist is required to complete a clinical preceptorship under the direct supervision of a dentist for a minimum of three months or 400 hours, whichever is longer.

56 Alaska Medicaid reimburses dental therapist services at the same encounter rate as services provided by a dentist.

57 K.A. Bolin, "Assessment of treatment provided by dental health aide therapists in Alaska; a pilot study," Journal of the American Dental Association, Vol. 139 (2008).

58 Scott Wetterhall MD, et al., Evaluation of the Dental Health Aide Therapist Workforce Model in Alaska (Research Triangle Park, N.C.: RTI International, October 2010).

59 2009 Minn. Laws Ch. 95, Art. 3.

60 In Minnesota, a dental therapist may perform a range of preventive and basic restorative procedures under remote consultative supervision of a dentist and intermediate restorative procedures under the on-site supervision of a dentist. Because of the on-site supervision requirement for intermediate restorative procedures, we do not consider Minnesota dental therapists as mid-level providers in this report.

61 The University of Minnesota School of Dentistry also offers a bachelor of science and a master's degree program which prepare students for licensure as dental therapists, but does not include the training required for advanced dental therapist certification.

62 Licensed dental therapists are also required to enter into consultative agreements.

63 Dental hygienists in Alabama may only perform dental procedures under the on-site supervision of a dentist. In addition to dental hygienists, dental assistants may provide a variety of services—depending on the state—including preventive and basic restorative procedures, however in general they require on-site supervision by a dentist.

64 In the remaining three states—Alabama, Alaska, and Mississippi—Medicaid covered services provided by dental hygienists are reimbursed through their supervising dentist.

65 Chris Cantrell, Engaging Primary Care Medical Providers in Children's Oral Health (Portland, Me.: National Academy for State Health Policy, September 2009). This study did not include a separate review of state CHIP reimbursement. According to officials from the Pew Center on the States, Children's Dental Campaign—the organization that funded the 2009 survey and monitors state Medicaid reimbursement policies—as of November 2010, 40 state Medicaid programs reimburse primary care medical providers for providing preventive dental procedures. Seven of the eight states we examined provided such reimbursement.

66 Pub. L. No. 111-148, § 5304, 124 Stat. 621. According to HRSA officials, as of June 2010, no funds had been appropriated specifically for these demonstration projects.

67 Rio Salado College is based in Tempe, Arizona.

68 The model proposed by the American Dental Hygienists' Association describes the supervisory arrangement for the advanced dental hygiene practitioner as a collaborative partnership with dentists for referral and consultations.

69 The countries are presented in chronological order by the date that their dental therapy programs started; New Zealand has the oldest dental therapy program. The United Kingdom consists of the countries of England, Northern Ireland, Scotland, and Wales.

70 These countries have other types of dental providers; however dental therapists are the only providers practicing in these countries who provide preventive, basic restorative and intermediate restorative dental procedures under remote supervision of a dentist. For example, Australia has a provider called a dental prosthesist who diagnoses and creates denture prosthesis, but does not provide primary (preventive and restorative) dental services.

71 Graduates of the combined programs are generally known as oral health therapists and are trained to provide dental hygiene services such as preventive teeth cleaning in addition to dental therapy services such as intermediate restorative tooth drilling.

72 The study examined 258 restorations on 80 adult patients six months after treatment. H. Calache, et. al, "The capacity of dental therapists to provide direct restorative care to adults," Australian and New Zealand Journal of Public Health, Vol. 33 (2009). An Australian official noted that the use of dental therapists is widely accepted and that because the programs are long-standing, few recent studies have been conducted. However, available research on the dental therapists in New Zealand (1951) and Canada (1974) showed that they provided restorative procedures that were similar in quality to restorative procedures provided by dentists.

73 Health officials from the United Kingdom reported that dental therapists have not had a major impact on children's access in the United Kingdom because patients must first see a dentist before being referred to a dental therapist.

74 The number of decayed, missing, or filled teeth calculated for both primary (baby) and permanent (adult) teeth is a common measure for dental disease experience. See J.M. Armfield and A.J. Spencer, "Quarter of a century of change: caries experience in Australian children, 1977-2002," Australian Dental Journal, Vol. 53 (2008).

75T he Saskatchewan school-based dental program was staffed by dental therapists and in existence from 1974 to 1993. D.W. Lewis, Performance of the Saskatchewan Health Dental Plan, 1974-1980, (University of Toronto, Toronto, Ontario, 1981). Although enrollment in the program by aboriginal children was much lower, enrollment of and access for these children increased over the period of study.

End Notes for Appendix I

1 ASTDD surveyed dental directors in all states and the District of Columbia. Respondents were asked to provide the most recent data available or data for the most recently completed fiscal year—generally 2008 data for the 2009 survey. See http://apps.nccd.cdc. gov/ synopses/ AboutV.asp (accessed July 21, 2010).

2 GAO/HEHS-00-149.

3 CHIPRA required that HHS post a complete and accurate list of dentists participating in state Medicaid and CHIP programs on the Insure Kids Now Web site by August 4, 2009. In June 2009, CMS issued guidance specifying certain data elements required for each dentist listed on the Insure Kids Now Web site, including the dentists' name, address, telephone number, and specialty; whether the dentist accepts new Medicaid or CHIP patients; and whether the dentist can accommodate patients with special needs.

4 For all 4 states, HHS's Insure Kids Now Web site allowed the user to enter a zip code to identify dentists nearest to the selected zip code.

5 The World Factbook 2009. Washington, D.C.: Central Intelligence Agency (2009). See https://www.cia.gov/library/publications/the-world-factbook/appendix/appendix-b.html#D (accessed Nov. 20, 2009).

6 We did not perform an independent review of laws and regulations of foreign jurisdictions, but relied on information provided by officials, government reports, and peer-reviewed research.

End Notes for Appendix III

1 H. R. Rep. No. 111-16, at 451 (2009) (Conf. Rep.).

2 Seventy-five-million dollars of the amount appropriated for NHSC is to remain available through September 30, 2011.

3 PPACA also authorized a total of approximately $31 billion for health centers for fiscal years 2011 through 2015, with authorization for funding in subsequent years to reflect the growth in costs and the number of patients served. However, these amounts remain unavailable for expenditure until appropriated.

4 PPACA established and authorized and appropriated funding to the Community Health Center Fund and directed amounts from this fund to be transferred to HHS to provide $9.5 billion in enhanced funding for health centers and $1.5 billion in enhanced funding for NHSC. It also authorized and appropriated $1.5 billion for construction and renovation of community health centers. Pub. L. No. 111-148, § 10503, 124 Stat. 1004, as amended by Pub. L. No. 111-152, § 2303, 134 Stat. 1083.

End Notes for Appendix V

1 U.S. Department of Health and Human Services, Indian Health Service, An Oral Health Survey of American Indian and Alaska Native Patients: Findings, Regional Differences and National Comparisons (Rockville, Md.).

2 The Alaska Tribal Health System operates using a four-tiered approach: (1) statewide services are provided in Anchorage, (2) regional services are provided at hubs within the various regions, (3) sub-regional clinics operate in some villages, and (4) small village clinics are where individuals obtain their primary health care.

3 The 2009 encounter data for one dental therapist was only for a portion of that year.

End Notes for Appendix VII

1 D.A. Nash, J.W. Friedman, T.B. Kardos, et al. "Dental Therapists: a global perspective," International Dental Journal, Vol. 58 (2008).

2 The countries are presented in chronological order by the date their dental therapist program started.

3 New Zealand pays for dental services for all children up to age 13, with most of the services provided by dental therapists in the school dental service.

4 Historically, dental therapists were trained in a 2-year non-degree granting program.

5 Dental therapists must be registered with the Dental Council of New Zealand—a self-regulating body for oral health professionals.

6 Dental therapists register for general dental therapy scope practice which allows practice for children up to age 18. Dental therapists can register for additional scopes of practice including adult care, radiology, and crowns.

7 K.M.S. Ayers, A. Meldrum, W.M. Thomson, J.T. Newton. "The working practices and career satisfaction of dental therapists in New Zealand," Community Dental Health, Vol. 24 (2007).

8 The United Kingdom consists of the countries of England, Northern Ireland, Scotland, and Wales. Each country has a National Health Service administered by Departments of Health that are responsible for administering health care. Countries in the United Kingdom have had subsidized dental services since the 1920s—known as the salaried dental service or community dental service—for which dental therapists were originally trained to serve.

9 Graduates of the combined programs can register as both a dental therapist and a dental hygienist. Historically, dental therapists were trained in 2-year hospital-based diploma programs, but since the 1990s programs have been offered through bachelor's degree granting programs.

10 The General Dental Council is the regulating body for oral health professionals.

11 The remaining dental therapists worked in hospitals, were teaching, or in a combination of positions. The National Health Service in each country contracts with independent dental practices—known as the general dental service—to provide services. Independent practices can be reimbursed by the National Health Service for dental services to children up to age 18.

12 J.H. Godson, J.S. Rowbotham, S.A. Williams, J.L. Csikar, S. Bradley, "Dental therapy in the United Kingdom: Part 2. a survey of reported working practices," British Dental Journal, Vol. 207 (2009).

13 All eight Australian states and territories subsidize dental care for children age 5-12, with certain states also paying for care to younger or older children.

14 Graduates of the combined programs are known as oral health therapists and can register as both a dental therapist and a dental hygienist. Historically, dental therapists were trained in 2-year non-bachelor degree granting programs.

15 Australian Institute of Health and Welfare, Dental Statistics and Research Unit, Dental Therapist Labour Force in Australia 2005 (Adelaide: Australia, July 2008).

16 Aboriginal populations in Canada are known as First Nations and Inuit. Health Canada— the government department responsible for administering health care—pays for dental services to all aboriginal populations. Private practices and tribes can be reimbursed by Health Canada for services rendered to those populations.

17 In the 1970s two provinces, Saskatchewan and later Manitoba, established school-based dental programs that utilized dental therapists to provide preventive and restorative dental services for children. The Saskatchewan program had high rates of enrollment and successfully reduced the rates of dental caries in children, and was privatized in 1987 and eliminated in 1993. Dental therapists that previously provided dental services in rural areas either moved to urban areas to work in private practice or lost their jobs according to a Canadian expert. D.W. Lewis, Performance of the Saskatchewan Health Dental Plan, 1974-1980. (Toronto: University of Toronto: 1981). The Manitoba program has also since been eliminated.

18 The Saskatchewan Dental Therapists Association is the self regulating body for dental therapists constituted under Saskatchewan law.

19 According to a Canadian health official, 52 dental therapists were employed directly by Health Canada and 30 were employed by First Nations tribes which are funded by Health Canada.

20 Dental therapists are not permitted to practice in Ontario or Quebec. In Manitoba, a number of dental therapists work in the private sector.

In: Child Health Care Support Programs ...   ISBN: 978-1-61470-970-1
Editors: W. Y. and X. Wen   © 2012 Nova Science Publishers, Inc.

Chapter 3

CHILDREN WITH DOWN SYNDROME: FAMILIES ARE MORE LIKELY TO RECEIVE RESOURCES AT TIME OF DIAGNOSIS THAN IN EARLY CHILDHOOD[*]

United States Government Accountability Office

WHY GAO DID THIS STUDY

On October 8, 2008, the Prenatally and Postnatally Diagnosed Conditions Awareness Act was signed into law, requiring GAO to submit a report concerning the effectiveness of current health care and family support programs for the families of children with disabilities. In this report, GAO focused on Down syndrome because it is a medical condition that is associated with disabilities and occurs frequently enough to yield a sufficient population size for an analysis.

GAO analyzed fee-for-service claims data from a very large private health insurance company, for the claims representing its experience with one of the largest national employers, and Medicaid claims data from seven states with high Medicaid enrollment and low percentages of enrollees in Medicaid managed care. GAO also interviewed specialists at six prominent Down

---

[*] This is an edited, reformatted and augmented version of the United States Government Accountability Office publication, Report to Congressional Committees GAO-11-57, dated October 2010.

syndrome clinics and 12 advocacy groups to examine what resources families receive and to identify barriers they face. GAO also analyzed data from the Health Resources and Services Administration–sponsored 2005-2006 National Survey of Children with Special Health Care Needs on barriers to accessing needed services.

WHAT GAO FOUND

GAO's analysis of data from a very large private health insurance company showed that from birth through early childhood, children with Down syndrome received medical care to address their special health care needs. Specifically, children with Down syndrome received, on average, five times more outpatient care (such as care in an urgent care facility) and over two times more office-based care (such as care in a physician's office) than children without Down syndrome. Overall, both groups received more office-based care than outpatient care. A key difference in the amount of care received by children with Down syndrome was the difference in the amount of therapy services, with a greater percentage of children with Down syndrome receiving physical, occupational, and speech therapy. In addition, children with Down syndrome have an increased risk of certain medical conditions and were hospitalized, on average, nearly twice as often and stayed twice as long as other children. Not surprisingly, differences were also found in medical care expenditures. The total average medical expenditures for children with Down syndrome were an average of five times higher than those for other children. However, both total expenditures and the difference in expenditures decreased substantially as the two groups of children reached 3 years of age. GAO's analysis of Medicaid claims data found similar differences between the two groups.

Down syndrome advocacy groups in selected communities told GAO that families of children with Down syndrome in those communities were more likely to receive the resources recommended for the time of diagnosis than those recommended for early childhood and may face barriers to using available resources. Specifically, advocacy groups reported that families were likely to receive about two-thirds (20 of 32) of the resources that specialists at the six Down syndrome clinics recommended they receive through their health care providers at the time of diagnosis. However, families were likely to receive only about one-quarter (6 of 23) of the resources that specialists recommended they receive through their health care providers after diagnosis and throughout early childhood. In addition, advocacy groups and results from the National Survey of Children with Special Health Care Needs indicate that families may face barriers that can prevent them from using available resources. For example, barriers such as outdated or inaccurate information could lead parents to underestimate their child's potential. Some advocacy groups reported that they and their communities have made efforts to address some of these barriers. For example, to address issues of inaccurate information, one advocacy group initiated an educational outreach program to health care professionals at area hospitals.

ABBREVIATIONS

AAP	American Academy of Pediatrics
ACMG	American College of Medical Genetics
ACOG	American Congress of Obstetricians and Gynecologists
DRG	diagnosis-related group
DSMIG	Down Syndrome Medical Interest Group
HHS	Department of Health and Human Services
HRSA	Health Resources and Services Administration
NDSC	National Down Syndrome Congress
NDSS	National Down Syndrome Society
NS-CSHCN	National Survey of Children with Special Health Care Needs
NSGC	National Society of Genetic Counselors

October 8, 2010
The Honorable Tom Harkin, Chairman
The Honorable Michael B. Enzi, Ranking Member
Committee on Health, Education, Labor, and Pensions, U. S. Senate

The Honorable Henry A. Waxman, Chairman
The Honorable Joe Barton, Ranking Member
Committee on Energy and Commerce,
House of Representatives

Families of children who have disabilities, such as children with Down syndrome, may not always receive the resources necessary to address their children's special health care needs. Down syndrome is a chromosomal condition that is associated with a set of cognitive and physical symptoms, and each year an estimated 1 in 733 babies is born with the condition in the United States.[1] Because of an increased risk of certain medical conditions, such as congenital heart defects, gastrointestinal problems, and thyroid disease, children with Down syndrome need timely medical care. According to advocates and Down syndrome specialists, early identification and treatment of health issues result in better health and increased capabilities for these children. In addition, families of children who have disabilities, such as children with Down syndrome, need certain resources—including information, programs, and referrals for specialty medical care—at the time of diagnosis and as their child ages so they can effectively work with their child's health care provider to identify and treat medical conditions early. However, research indicates that not all families get the help they need. For example, researchers have consistently found that families reported both a lack of support and a lack of accurate information from their physicians at the time of diagnosis and as the child ages.[2]

On October 8, 2008, the Prenatally and Postnatally Diagnosed Conditions Awareness Act was signed into law to increase the provision of scientifically sound information and support services to patients receiving a positive test diagnosis for Down syndrome or other prenatally and postnatally diagnosed conditions.[3] This act required GAO to submit a report concerning the effectiveness of current health care and family support programs for the families of children with disabilities. In this report, we focused on Down syndrome because it is the most commonly occurring chromosomal condition at birth and, therefore, occurs frequently enough to yield sufficient population size for an analysis. Moreover, physicians with experience treating children with Down syndrome and children who have other disabilities reported that many of the health care issues and experiences faced by families of children with Down syndrome are similar to those faced by families of children who have other disabilities. In this report, we examined (1) what is known about the extent to which children diagnosed with Down syndrome receive medical care during early childhood and (2) what resources families of children with Down syndrome receive through their health care providers and what barriers families face to using these resources.

To determine what is known about the extent to which children diagnosed with Down syndrome receive medical care during early childhood,[4] we analyzed fee-for-service claims data from a very large private health insurance company for the claims representing its experience with one of the largest national employers. We also analyzed Medicaid fee-for-service claims data from seven states.[5] We obtained the most recent full years of claims data available from each source. From the private health insurance company, we received nationwide claims data from 2001 through 2008, and from Medicaid, we received claims data from seven states for 2007.[6] To select the seven states, we chose states with high Medicaid enrollment and low percentages of enrollees in Medicaid managed care; in 2006, the seven states accounted for over 40 percent of all Medicaid enrollees nationwide. For each 1-year period from birth through age 4, we analyzed claims data for children with Down syndrome[7] who were enrolled in the private health insurance company or Medicaid for at least 11 months of that period.[8] Specifically, we analyzed data on claims for outpatient, inpatient, and office-based care[9] to describe the medical care received by children with Down syndrome during early childhood and corresponding health care expenditures. To provide a point of reference, we analyzed similar data for children without Down syndrome.[10] The results of these analyses are not generalizable to all children with or without Down syndrome. We discussed the reliability of these data sources with knowledgeable officials and performed data reliability checks, such as examining the data for missing values and obvious errors, to test the internal consistency and reliability of the data. After taking these steps, we determined that the data were sufficiently reliable for our purposes.

To determine what resources families of children with Down syndrome receive through their health care providers and what barriers families face to using these resources, we conducted a series of interviews with national Down syndrome organizations and national disability organizations, specialists at Down syndrome clinics,[11] and Down syndrome advocacy groups.[12] Specifically, we interviewed 10 national Down syndrome organizations and national disability organizations and asked them to identify prominent Down syndrome clinics known for their expertise in treating children with Down syndrome. From these 10 interviews, we selected the six most commonly cited Down syndrome clinics[13] and asked specialists at each of these clinics to recommend the resources families should receive through their health care providers both at diagnosis and through early childhood.[14] We then selected 12 Down syndrome advocacy groups, representing six communities across the country, each of which was located in the same state as one of the six Down syndrome clinics. We asked the Down syndrome advocacy groups to review the list of resources that the specialists recommended and comment on whether families in their communities were likely to have received those resources through their health care providers. We also asked the Down syndrome advocacy groups to identify barriers families face to using the resources in their communities. The results of these interviews cannot be generalized to all Down syndrome clinics, all Down syndrome advocacy groups, or all families of children with Down syndrome.

To supplement our work, we obtained information from the National Survey of Children with Special Health Care Needs (NS-CSHCN), 2005-2006, which is sponsored by the Health Resources and Services Administration (HRSA).[15] Specifically, we obtained the most recent data available on issues such as access to health care, impact of special health care needs on the family, and barriers to accessing needed services. We analyzed survey data for families of children with Down syndrome from birth through age 17.[16] The survey was designed to be representative of the entire U.S. population.[17] We reviewed relevant data reliability materials and performed data reliability checks, such as examining the data for missing values and obvious errors, to test the internal consistency and reliability of the data. After taking these steps, we determined that the data were sufficiently reliable for our purposes.

We conducted this performance audit from November 2009 to October 2010 in accordance with generally accepted government auditing standards. Those standards require that we plan and perform the audit to obtain sufficient, appropriate evidence to provide a reasonable basis for our findings and conclusions based on our audit objectives. We believe that the evidence obtained provides a reasonable basis for our findings and conclusions based on our audit objectives.

BACKGROUND

Overview of Down Syndrome

Down syndrome is most frequently caused by a chromosomal error that produces an extra copy of chromosome 21.[18] The extra chromosomal material causes children with Down syndrome to have mental[19] and physical differences and a greater risk of developing certain medical problems, such as hearing loss, eye disease, and congenital heart defects. (See table 1.) Because of this heightened risk, the American Academy of Pediatrics recommends that children with Down syndrome be closely screened throughout childhood for certain medical conditions.

**Table 1. Occurrence of Other Medical Conditions
among Children with Down Syndrome**

Medical condition	Percentage of children with Down syndrome who have condition
Hearing loss	75
Eye disease	60
Congenital heart defects	50
Otitis media[a]	50-70
Obstructive sleep apnea	50-75
Thyroid disease	15
Gastrointestinal atresias[b]	12
Acquired hip dislocation	6
Leukemia	<1
Hirschsprung disease[c]	<1

Source: GAO analysis of American Academy of Pediatrics data in *Health Supervision for Children with Down Syndrome* (February 2001).

Note: Children with Down syndrome have a higher risk for developing these medical conditions than children without Down syndrome.

[a] Otitis media is an infection or inflammation of the middle ear.

[b] A gastrointestinal atresia is a complete blockage or obstruction in the gastrointestinal tract.

[c] Hirschsprung disease is a blockage of the large intestine caused by improper muscle movement in the bowel.

Families of Children with Down Syndrome

The overall well-being of some families of children with Down syndrome can be affected by the special needs that their children may have. Research shows that these families experience more stress than families of typically developing children.[20] In addition, according to the NS-CSHCN, 21 percent of families of children from birth through age 17 with Down syndrome in the United States needed mental health care or family counseling in the previous year, and 26 percent experienced financial problems as a result of their child's health care issues.[21] Research shows that families can benefit from family support resources, such as parent support groups where information and stories can be informally exchanged. In fact, connecting a new parent to other parents, such as through a parent support group, has been shown to be among the most helpful resources a physician can provide during the first conversation.[22]

Research has shown that families of children with Down syndrome do not receive enough accurate information and emotional support at the time of diagnosis and as the child ages.[23] A 2005 study that surveyed 985 mothers who received a postnatal diagnosis of Down syndrome for their children indicated that when they learned of their child's diagnosis their physicians had not provided them with a satisfactory amount of up-to-date printed materials or telephone numbers of parents who already had a child with Down syndrome.[24] Another study found that families received some information from health care providers that they perceived as vague, inaccurate, or outdated.[25] Although there are studies such as these and other initiatives[26] that focus on the first conversation between the health care provider and the family, there is very little research addressing subsequent conversations between the health care provider and the family as the child ages.

Down Syndrome Clinics, Programs, and Advocacy Groups

Down syndrome clinics, which are usually located in larger cities across the United States, are a source of specialty medical care for children with Down syndrome.[27] Pediatricians and family physicians vary widely in terms of their experience treating children with Down syndrome and refer patients to Down syndrome clinics as needed. The Down syndrome clinics are typically associated with medical schools or large hospitals and may include geneticists, developmental pediatricians, therapists, nutritionists, nurse practitioners, and genetic counselors. Families may visit these clinics on an annual basis to assess their child's development and to ensure that any health conditions have been properly diagnosed.[28] Families of children with multiple medical problems may visit these clinics more frequently to ensure that their child is receiving appropriate specialty care. In addition to caring for children, these clinics also support families by, for example, providing information about Down syndrome and referring families to community resources.

Pediatricians may also recommend that children with Down syndrome be referred to early intervention programs in their area. Children with Down syndrome qualify for early intervention services—which are generally administered by state-level agencies—beginning at birth and continuing until the age of 3.[29] The Individuals with Disabilities Education Act Part C program was created to provide infants and toddlers who have disabilities (or are at risk of developing a disability) and their families with early intervention services, such as speech therapy, occupational therapy, and family counseling.[30] We previously reported on research that found that the earlier a child with disabilities receives early intervention services, the more effective these services may be in enhancing the child's development. [31] Parents may be referred to early intervention programs by their child's doctor, or they may seek out these services themselves.

There is also a widespread network of advocacy groups to support children with Down syndrome and their families. In addition to numerous national disability organizations, there are two national Down syndrome-specific organizations with over 300 local advocacy groups located across the country. They range in size from small parent support groups to larger organizations that provide services to families and their children. Advocacy groups support children with Down syndrome and their families by, for example, organizing activities for children, serving as information resources, and offering parent support groups.

CHILDREN WITH DOWN SYNDROME RECEIVED MEDICAL CARE TO ADDRESS SPECIAL HEALTH CARE NEEDS

Children with Down Syndrome Received More Outpatient and Office-Based Care than Other Children, with Number of Therapy Services a Key Difference

From birth through early childhood, children with Down syndrome received, on average, five times more outpatient care and over two times more office-based care than children without Down syndrome,[32] according to our analysis of data from a private health insurance company.[33] For children under 1 year of age,[34] the average number of outpatient services was 10.4 for children with Down syndrome and 1.9 for children without. Similarly, the average number of office-based services for children under 1 year of age was 20.0 for children with Down syndrome and 10.7 for children without. As children with and without Down syndrome moved through early childhood, both groups received more office-based services than outpatient services.[35]

However, while the amounts of outpatient and office-based services decreased over time, the differences in the amounts of outpatient and office-based services between the two groups remained. (See fig. 1.)

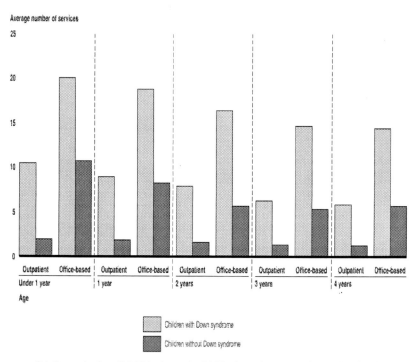

Source: GAO analysis of 2001 through 2008 data from a private health insurance company for the claims representing its experience with one of the largest national employers.

Notes: Outpatient care includes services received in facilities such as urgent care facilities, ambulatory surgical centers, and hospital emergency rooms. Office-based care includes services received in facilities such as physician offices, community health clinics, and school-based health clinics. Some services, such as therapy, can be provided in different types of facilities. For this analysis, we classified each service as outpatient care or office-based care based on the type of facility in which it was provided. The age ranges in our analysis are constructed so that, for example, "under 1 year" includes all children from birth up to but not including their first birthday, and so on, with each range consisting of 1 full year.

Figure 1. Average Number of Outpatient and Office-Based Services Received by Children in Our Review, by Age.

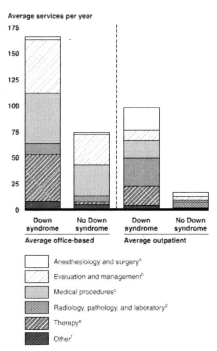

Source: GAO analysis of 2001 through 2008 data from a private health insurance
    company for the claims representing its experience with one of the largest national
    employers.
Notes: Outpatient care includes services received in facilities such as urgent care
    facilities, ambulatory surgical centers, and hospital emergency rooms. Office-
    based care includes services received in facilities such as physician offices,
    community health clinics, and school-based health clinics. Some services, such as
    therapy, can be provided in different types of facilities. For this analysis, we
    classified each service as outpatient care or office-based care based on the type of
    facility in which it was provided.
[a] Anesthesiology surgery includes services as ear drum openings and wound repairs.
[b] Evaluation and management includes services such as office, outpatient, and
    emergency department visits.
[c] Medical procedures includes services such as vaccinations, hearing tests, cardiac tests.
[d] Radiology, pathology, laboratory includes services such as thyroid tests, chest X-rays.
[e] Therapy includes services such as physical, occupational, and speech therapy.
[f] Other includes services such as dental services that are not captured in the other
    categories.

Figure 2. Average Number of Outpatient and Office-Based Services Received by
Children in Our Review from Birth through Age 4, by Service Type.

Across all types of services, children with Down syndrome from birth through age 4 received more outpatient and office-based services than children without. (See fig. 2.) For example, for both outpatient and office-based services, children with Down syndrome had more evaluation and management services,[36] more medical procedure services, and more therapy services. Specifically, for outpatient services, children with Down syndrome had 3 times more evaluation and management services, 10 times more medical procedure services, and 22 times more therapy services than children without. For office-based services, children with Down syndrome had 2 times more evaluation and management services, 2 times more medical procedure services, and 25 times more office-based therapy services than children without. In addition, children with Down syndrome had 6 times more outpatient anesthesiology and surgery services than children without.[37]

We found other differences within the types of services received, such as greater percentages of children with Down syndrome receiving services such as thyroid, cardiac, and hearing tests than other children. For example, our review of the outpatient services found that 21 percent of children with Down syndrome under 1 year of age had a specific thyroid function test, compared to 1 percent of other children of the same age.[38] In addition, children with Down syndrome were more likely than other children to receive an influenza vaccination; for example, 30 percent of 4- year-olds with Down syndrome received the influenza vaccine, compared to 15 percent of other children of the same age.

A key difference in the amount of outpatient and office-based care received by children with Down syndrome and other children was the difference in the amount of therapy services received. Our analysis of therapy usage showed that the percentage of children with Down syndrome who received physical, occupational, and speech therapy— therapies that Down syndrome specialists say are important for children with Down syndrome to receive to maximize their development—was much higher than it was for other children.[39] For example, 50 percent of children with Down syndrome, birth through age 4, received physical therapy services, compared to 3 percent of other children. This represented an average of 30 physical therapy claims per child with Down syndrome, compared to an average of less than 1 physical therapy claim per child without. This difference in the amount of children who received therapy services was evident in each age group and for each therapy type. (See fig. 3.)

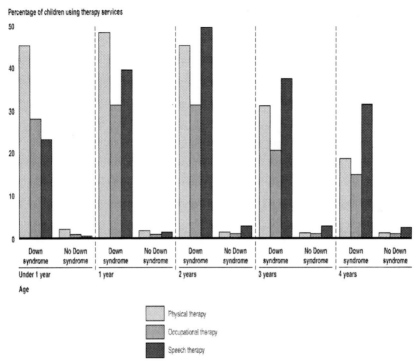

Percentage of children using therapy services

Source: GAO analysis of 2001 through 2008 data from a private health insurance company for the claims representing its experience with one of the largest national employers.

Note: The age ranges in our analysis are constructed so that, for example, "under 1 year" includes all children from birth up to but not including their first birthday, and so on, with each range consisting of 1 full year.

Figure 3. Percentage of Children in Our Review Using Therapy Services, by Age and Therapy Type.

The Medicaid data that we reviewed from seven states also show that children from birth through age 4 with Down syndrome who were enrolled in Medicaid in 2007 received more outpatient and office-based care to address their special health care needs than other children of the same age.[40] For example, among the seven states, children with Down syndrome received 2.7 to 5.3 times more outpatient services and 1.6 to 4.5 times more office-based services than children without Down syndrome. (See app. I for more Medicaid data.)

Children with Down Syndrome Were Hospitalized More Frequently and Had Longer Hospital Stays than Other Children

According to our analysis of inpatient care[41] data from a large private health insurance company, from birth through early childhood, children with Down syndrome were hospitalized, on average, nearly twice as often and stayed twice as long as children without Down syndrome.[42] The differences in the average number of hospitalizations and the average length of stay were most pronounced in the first years of life and diminished by age 4. (See figs. 4 and 5.)

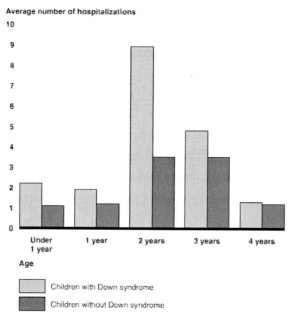

Source: GAO analysis of 2001 through 2008 data from a private health insurance company for the claims representing its experience with one of the largest national employers.

Notes: The increase in hospitalizations for children 2 years of age with Down syndrome may be a result of physicians waiting to address certain health issues—such as some ear, nose, and throat issues—until children are older. The age ranges in our analysis are constructed so that, for example, "under 1 year" includes all children from birth up to but not including their first birthday, and so on, with each range consisting of 1 full year.

Figure 4. Average Number of Hospitalizations of Children in Our Review, by Age.

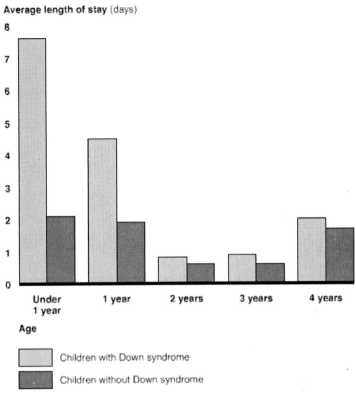

Figure 5. Average Length of Hospital Stay of Children in Our Review, by Age.

Note: The age ranges in our analysis are constructed so that, for example, "under 1 year" includes all children from birth up to but not including their first birthday, and so on, with each range consisting of 1 full year.

For example, for children with Down syndrome under 1 year of age, the average number of hospitalizations was 2.2, and the average length of stay was 7.6 days. In contrast, for children of the same age without Down syndrome, the average number of hospitalizations was 1.1, and the average length of stay was 2.1 days.[43] In an older group—children 4 years of age—children with and without Down syndrome were hospitalized about the same number of times, an average of 1.3 times for children with Down syndrome and an average of 1.2 times for children without, and for about the same length of time, an average of 2.0 days for children with Down syndrome and 1.7 days for children without.

Our review of inpatient claims data showed some differences in the types of hospitalizations for children with Down syndrome compared to other children.[44] For example, the most common type of hospitalization for children with Down syndrome under 1 year of age was cardiothoracicrelated surgery; 6 percent of children under 1 year of age with Down syndrome had this hospital-ization type, compared to 0.03 percent of other children.[45] Furthermore, while other hospitalization types—such as bronchitis and asthma, pneumonia, and ear issues—appeared as common types of hospital-izations in both groups, the percentage of children with Down syndrome hospitalized for these reasons was higher.

The Medicaid data that we reviewed from seven states also show that children from birth through age 4 with Down syndrome who were enrolled in Medicaid in 2007 generally had more inpatient care. Children with Down syndrome had more hospitalizations (in six of the seven states) and longer hospital stays to address their special health care needs than other children of the same age.[46] For example, among the seven states, children with Down syndrome had 1.0 to 7.4 times more hospitalizations and 1.5 to 10.2 times longer stays than children without Down syndrome. (See app. I for more Medicaid data.)

Children with Down Syndrome Had Higher Average Medical Care Expenditures than Other Children, with Differences Decreasing as Children Aged

In our review, the total average medical expenditures[47] for children with Down syndrome, from birth through early childhood, were an average of five times higher than the expenditures for children without Down syndrome;[48] however, both total expenditures and the difference in expenditures decreased substantially by the time children with Down syndrome were 3 years of age. (See fig. 6.) The expenditures were also higher for children with Down syndrome for each type of medical care— outpatient, office-based, and inpatient care. Inpatient care for children under 1 year of age had the greatest difference, with average expenditures of almost $43,000 for children with Down syndrome and $2,000 for children without. The difference in expenditures reflects the fact that children with Down syndrome had a higher utilization of medical care or more expensive medical services than children without Down syndrome.

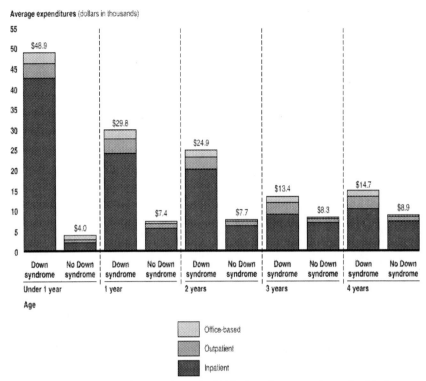

Source: GAO analysis of 2001 through 2008 data from a private health insurance
company for the claims representing its experience with one of the largest national
employers.

Notes: Office-based care includes services received in facilities such as physician
offices, community health clinics, and school-based health clinics. Outpatient care
includes services received in facilities such as urgent care facilities, ambulatory
surgical centers, and hospital emergency rooms. Inpatient care includes services
received in residential health care facilities such as hospitals. Some services, such
as therapy, can be provided in different types of facilities. For this analysis, we
classified each service as outpatient care, office-based care, or inpatient care based
on the type of facility in which it was provided. Expenditure data were adjusted to
2008 dollars and include the amount paid by the primary insurance company, the
deductible, coinsurance, and the amount paid by secondary insurance. The age
ranges in our analysis are constructed so that, for example, "under 1 year"
includes all children from birth up to but not including their first birthday, and so on, with
each range consisting of 1 full year.

Figure 6. Average Expenditures for Outpatient, Office-Based, and Inpatient Services
for Children in Our Review, by Age.

FAMILIES WERE MORE LIKELY TO RECEIVE THE RESOURCES RECOMMENDED FOR TIME OF DIAGNOSIS THAN THOSE RECOMMENDED FOR EARLY CHILDHOOD, AND MAY FACE BARRIERS TO USING AVAILABLE RESOURCES

Families Were Likely to Receive Many, but Not All, of the Resources that Down Syndrome Clinic Specialists Recommended They Receive at Diagnosis

Down syndrome advocacy groups in selected communities told us that families in those communities were likely to receive many, but not all, of the resources that Down syndrome clinic specialists recommended they receive at the time of diagnosis. The specialists from six Down syndrome clinics we interviewed recommended 32 resources. (See table 2.) Advocacy groups reported that families were likely to receive about two-thirds (20 of 32) of the recommended resources; these resources were generally directly related to the health of children with Down syndrome, such as information about the risk of cardiac problems and the need for thyroid screening. Families were less likely to receive about one-third (10 of 32) of the recommended resources; these resources were generally related to the family's understanding of Down syndrome and overall family well-being, such as a copy of the Down syndrome-specific health care guidelines[49] and information about the causes of Down syndrome and the effect of Down syndrome on the family and caregivers.[50]

The time of diagnosis is a key time for children with Down syndrome and their families. According to the Down syndrome clinic specialists, if newborns are not tested for certain medical conditions immediately after diagnosis, serious and even life-threatening consequences can occur. In addition, specialists from one Down syndrome clinic noted that this is a key time for families to be given information to help them understand how their child's diagnosis may affect their family.

However, according to the Down syndrome clinic specialists, families can be overwhelmed if too much information is presented at the time of diagnosis, especially if they are already overwhelmed emotionally and psychologically from receiving the diagnosis.

Table 2. Resources That Specialists from Six Down Syndrome Clinics Recommended Families Receive Immediately upon Diagnosis, Likelihood of Receipt, and Consequences If Not Received

Recommended resources	Twelve advocacy groups' assessment of likelihood of receipt by families	Consequences Down syndrome clinic specialists reported if resource not received
Information about:		
Need to screen for cardiac problems	•	If the child is not screened, serious complications or death in the first days or weeks of life may occur.
Need to perform echocardiogram[a]	•	If not performed, a congenital heart problem could go undiagnosed, and serious complications or death may occur.
Need for thyroid screening[b]	•	If the child is not screened, hypothyroidism may not be detected, and permanent cognitive impairment, along with growth and metabolic issues, may occur.
Need for complete blood count screening	•	If the child is not screened, early signs of leukemia may go undetected.
Need for hearing screening[c]	•	If the child is not screened, problems such as impaired language development or permanent hearing loss may occur.
Need for vaccines (following standard schedule)	•	If the child is not vaccinated, severe illness due to delayed immune system maturity may occur.
Impact of low muscle tone (e.g., for feeding, walking)	•	If not received, families may not understand the need for interventions such as therapy services, which can help improve feeding and gross and fine motor skills, such as learning how to sit, crawl, stand, and walk.
Potential for gastrointestinal problems	•	If not informed, families may be unaware that the child can experience complications such as an intestinal obstruction, which may be lifethreatening.
Potential need for referrals to pediatric specialists	•	If families do not access a specialist when care is needed, conditions may go undiagnosed or untreated.

Table 2. (Continued).

Recommended resources	Twelve advocacy groups' assessment of likelihood of receipt by families	Consequences Down syndrome clinic specialists reported if resource not received
Potential developmental delays	●	If families are not prepared for potential developmental delays, such as delayed speech, they may have unrealistic expectations of their child and experience additional stress and confusion.
Most medical issues for children with Down syndrome being treatable	●	If not received, families may experience unnecessary stress and anxiety about their child's health and well-being.
Need for therapy services (e.g., occupational and speech therapy)	●	If not received, the child may not have appropriate therapies and may develop maladaptive behaviors.
Likelihood for Down syndrome recurrence (e.g., check karyotype[d])	●	If not received, parents may be unaware that their child has a rare, inherited form of Down syndrome.
Breast feeding support resources	●	If not received, child may have difficulty feeding—especially sucking and swallowing— which can affect growth.
Overview of health issues that are likely to occur in the first year or two of life	●	If families do not receive this information, they may be unaware of what conditions their child is at risk for developing and what symptoms they should look for.
Referral to early intervention program in their area	●	If this referral is not received, developmental delays cannot be addressed and monitored and the child may develop maladaptive behaviors.
Referral to meet with a genetic counselor	●	If not received, family may not benefit from the expertise of a genetic counselor, who can discuss the cause of Down syndrome and any related health concerns.

Contact information for local Down syndrome support groups	●	If not received, families may not benefit from learning about the experiences of other families and may face difficulties, such as feeling isolated, which may affect their ability to care for their child with Down syndrome or their other children.
Contact information for a Down syndrome clinic (if available in their area)	●	If not received, child or family may not benefit from the specialized resources of a Down syndrome clinic, if needed.
Additional support (e.g., social workers) to families whose babies have long hospital stays	●	If not received, families may experience higher stress levels, which could affect their ability to care for their child with Down syndrome or their other children.
Information about:		
When child's first early intervention[c] visit should occur	○	If families are not informed that the first visit should occur within the first few weeks or months of birth, they may delay accessing this important resource.
Importance of mother and infant bonding	○	If families are not informed of the importance of this bonding and the mother is struggling to bond with her infant, she may experience depression and anxiety, which can have repercussions for the health of the child if it continues over a long period of time.
Causes of Down syndrome	○	If not received, families without information or with inaccurate information may struggle to cope with diagnosis and understand their child.
Effect of Down syndrome on family and caregivers	○	If not received, family members may experience stress and develop feelings of isolation.
Sibling support resources	○	If not received, siblings may experience stress and develop feelings of isolation that could affect long-term family well-being.

Table 2. (Continued).

Recommended resources	Twelve advocacy groups' assessment of likelihood of receipt by families	Consequences Down syndrome clinic specialists reported if resource not received
Sources for accurate, up-to-date Down syndrome information	○	If families do not receive accurate, up-to-date Down syndrome information, they may not be informed aadvocates for their child and family as they negotiate the health care system.
Importance of enjoying time with baby	○	If families are not informed of the importance of enjoying their baby, they may focus more on the Down syndrome diagnosis than on their new baby.
Financial assistance resources (e.g., advisor, public insurance)	○	If families do not receive this information, they may be unaware of the long-term financial planning needs of their child with Down syndrome or the insurance coverage that their child can access.
Contact information for national Down syndrome groups	○	If not received, families may not access important resources that can help with stress and feelings of isolation.
Copy of health care guidelines for children with Down syndrome (e.g., those from AAP and/or DSMIG[f])	○	If not received, families may not be fully aware of the health risks their child may face and, as a result, may be less effective advocates.
Information about what Down syndrome is	⊙	If not received, families may have inaccurate information, which may affect how they understand and cope with the diagnosis and advocate for their child.

Additional support to families who ask for help talking about Down syndrome diagnosis	⊙	If not received, families may experience confusion, anxiety, and isolation because they do not know how to cope with the diagnosis and convey their child's diagnosis to people in their social networks.

Source: GAO.

• The majority of the 12 advocacy groups we interviewed reported that these resources were likely to be received.

O The majority of the 12 advocacy groups we interviewed reported that these resources were less likely to be received.

⊙ Half of the 12 advocacy groups we interviewed reported that these resources were likely to be received, and half reported that these were less likely to be received.

Note: According to the Down syndrome clinic specialists, some of the resources in this table should be received by families at the time of diagnosis and again throughout the child's life.

[a] An echocardiogram is a test that uses sound waves to create a moving picture of the heart.

[b] Newborns across the United States are universally screened for thyroid problems at birth.

[c] Newborns in most states are universally screened for hearing problems at birth.

[d] A karyotype is a test to examine the chromosomes in a sample of cells.

[e] Early intervention programs, which are generally administered by state-level agencies, provide infants and toddlers (ages 0 to 3) who have a disability, or who are at risk of developing a disability, and their families with appropriate services, such as speech therapy, occupational therapy, and family counseling.

[f] Both the American Academy of Pediatrics (AAP) and the Down Syndrome Medical Interest Group (DSMIG) have published Down syndrome-specific health care guidelines for physicians. These guidelines for physicians contain many of the same health items that are on this list.

All of the specialists we interviewed at the six Down syndrome clinics agreed that if families do not receive resources recommended for the time of diagnosis, the health consequences for the child could be severe. For example, if a newborn's heart defect is not detected early, he or she may experience serious complications and even death in the first days or weeks of life. If a newborn's hypothyroidism[51]—which can be easily treated—is not detected early, he or she may experience additional cognitive impairment or other complications. If a family is not provided with a copy of the Down syndrome-specific health care guidelines, they may not be fully aware of the health risks their child may face, and they may be less effective advocates. (See table 2 for these and other health consequences that may occur if these resources are not received by families.)

Advocacy groups told us that if there were gaps in the resources that families received from their health care providers upon diagnosis, advocacy groups and other community organizations sometimes provided the missing material. For example, advocacy groups sometimes drop off "New Parent Packets" at area hospitals that include the Down syndrome-specific health care guidelines and information about what Down syndrome is and how it can affect the family. Advocacy groups also offer family support groups, including groups geared specifically toward grandparents and fathers, and host seminars on financial planning.

Families Were Less Likely to Receive Most of the Resources that Down Syndrome Clinic Specialists Recommended for Early Childhood

In contrast to the time of diagnosis, Down syndrome advocacy groups in selected communities told us that families of children with Down syndrome in those communities were less likely to receive most of the recommended resources from their health care providers for early childhood. These resources are important to their children's ongoing health and the well-being of their families. The specialists from six Down syndrome clinics we interviewed recommended 23 resources that families should receive through their health care providers after diagnosis and throughout early childhood. (See table 3.) Advocacy groups reported that families were likely to receive only about one-quarter (6 of 23) of these resources. For example, resources that families were likely to receive included information about the need to screen for celiac disease, the need for vision screening, and the risk for upper respiratory infections. But families were less likely to receive about three-quarters (17 of 23) of the resources recommended for early childhood. For example, families were less likely to receive information about the need to see a pediatric dentist, how to prevent obesity, and the importance of communicating with their child. In addition, families were less likely to receive a copy of a Down syndrome-specific growth chart.

Table 3. Resources Important to the Ongoing Health of the Child That Specialists from Six Down Syndrome Clinics Recommended Families Receive for Early Childhood, Likelihood of Receipt, and Consequences If Not Received

Recommended resources	Twelve advocacy groups' assessment of likelihood of receipt by families	Consequences Down syndrome clinic specialists reported if resource not received
Information about:		
Need for vision screening	●	If the child is not screened, an undiagnosed impairment may delay vision development and may cause permanent blindness.
Need for celiac disease screening[a]	●	If the child is not screened, undiagnosed celiac disease may affect the child's growth and cause problems such as diarrhea, constipation, and behavioral changes.
Need for cervical spine screening[b]	●	If the child is not screened, undiagnosed movement of the cervical spine may lead to serious or permanent damage to the spinal cord.
Need to perform neck X-ray	●	If the child is not screened, undiagnosed movement of the cervical spine may lead to serious or permanent damage to the spinal cord.
Need to perform neurological examination[c]	●	If the child is not screened, undiagnosed movement of the cervical spine may lead to serious or permanent damage to the spinal cord.
Risk for upper respiratory infections	●	If not informed, families may not be aware that upper respiratory issues need to be treated quickly to prevent more serious illness.

Table 3. (Continued).

Recommended resources	Twelve advocacy groups' assessment of likelihood of receipt by families	Consequences Down syndrome clinic specialists reported if resource not received
Need for more doctor visits for child with Down syndrome	○	If not received, families may be surprised and unprepared for the frequent referrals to specialists and the need for follow-up appointments.
Need to see a pediatric dentist	○	If not received, families may be unaware that children with Down syndrome have a high risk for dental problems, such as missing or crowded teeth.
Potential for infantile spasms[d]	○	If not informed, the parents may not recognize the symptoms, which might lead to additional developmental delays.
Recommended resources	Twelve advocacy groups' assessment of likelihood of receipt by families	Consequences Down syndrome clinic specialists reported if resource not received
Potential sleeping issues	○	If not informed, families may be unaware that sleeping issues, particularly obstructive sleep apnea and sleep disturbances, can lead to chronic cardiopulmonary disease as well as problems with attention, behavior, and learning.
Potential use of Synagis vaccine[e] (e.g., for respiratory illness)	○	If not informed, at-risk children may not be vaccinated and can develop respiratory syncytial virus, which can cause illnesses ranging from the common cold to a very severe illness, and even death.

Potential sensory processing disorders[f]	○	If not informed, families may be unaware that children with Down syndrome can develop sensitivities such as those related to food texture, touch, and sound, which can lead to behavior that further complicates development.
Physical activity and proper nutrition to prevent obesity	○	If not informed, families may be unaware that the child can develop obesity and associated medical conditions, such as type II diabetes and blood pressure problems. Lack of physical activity affects other health issues, such as energy levels, sleep, and mental health.
Transition that occurs at age 3 from early intervention[g] to school system	○	If not informed, parents may not place their child in the most appropriate educational setting.
Importance of communicating with child (e.g., sign language)	○	If not informed, families may not use early communication techniques, which may lead to frustration and behavioral problems.
Learning styles for children with Down syndrome (e.g., visual learners)	○	If not informed, parents may not learn about educational techniques that work well for children with Down syndrome.
What it is like to grow up with Down syndrome	○	If not received, families may have inaccurate information, which may affect how they cope with the diagnosis, approach parenting, and understand what is possible for their child.

Table 3. (Continued).

Recommended resources	Twelve advocacy groups' assessment of likelihood of receipt by families	Consequences Down syndrome clinic specialists reported if resource not received
National conferences where families can network and get information	○	If not received, families may miss an opportunity to interact with other people with Down syndrome and their families and gather important information.
Support groups for comorbidities/dual diagnoses, if needed (e.g., autism)	○	If not received, families of children with dual diagnoses may feel excluded from Down syndrome-only support groups and experience feelings of isolation.
The Special Olympics[h]	○	If not received, children may not participate in the Special Olympics; programs such as this help physical development, which is important for mental health and weight management.
Social development opportunities in the community (e.g., playgroups)	○	If not received, children with Down syndrome may miss the opportunity to practice speech and language, model behaviors, and develop social skills.
Non-Down syndrome community resources for children	○	If not received, children with Down syndrome may not feel integrated into their community and could miss out on these social development opportunities.
Copy of a Down syndrome-specific growth chart[i]	○	If not received, families may not have an understanding of the growth expectations for their child and how they differ from the typical growth chart.

- The majority of the 12 advocacy groups we interviewed reported that these resources were likely to be received.
○ The majority of the 12 advocacy groups we interviewed reported that these resources were less likely to be received.

Note: Both the American Academy of Pediatrics (AAP) and the Down Syndrome Medical Interest Group (DSMIG) have published Down syndrome-specific health care guidelines for physicians. These guidelines for physicians contain many of the same items that are on this list.

[a] Celiac disease causes a reaction to eating gluten, which damages the lining of the small intestine and prevents the intestine from absorbing food.

[b] A cervical spine screening can detect increased mobility of the cervical spine, a condition also referred to as atlantoaxial instability.

[c] A neurological examination uses a series of questions and tests to check the brain, spinal cord, and nerve function. The examination also checks mental status, coordination, and the functioning of muscles, senses, and reflexes.

[d] Infantile spasms are a type of seizure seen in infancy and childhood that causes a sudden bending forward of the body with a stiffening of the arms and legs.

[e] Synagis is a Food and Drug Administration-approved medication to help protect young babies from respiratory syncytial virus, a common virus that can be serious and, in some cases, can cause death.

[f] Sensory processing disorders are characterized by over- or undersensitivity to environmental stimuli.

[g] Early intervention programs, which are generally administered by state-level agencies, provide infants and toddlers (ages 0 to 3) who have disabilities, or who are at risk of developing a disability, and their families with appropriate services, such as speech therapy, occupational therapy, and family counseling.

[h] The Special Olympics is an organization and competition for people who have intellectual disabilities and guides local, national, and international programs. Children with intellectual disabilities between the ages of 2 through 7 can participate in the Youth Athletes program, and children with intellectual disabilities ages 8 and older can become Special Olympics athletes.

[i] C. Cronk et al. "Growth Charts for Children with Down Syndrome: 1 Month to 18 Years of Age," *Pediatrics*, vol. 81, no. 1 (1988).

According to the Down syndrome clinic specialists, some information is most useful if provided in early childhood rather than at the time of diagnosis. For example, information about celiac disease is not necessary at diagnosis because it usually is not detectable until the child has begun eating solid foods.

According to the clinic specialists, if families do not receive the resources recommended for early childhood, there may be health consequences for the child. For example, if a child's poor vision is not detected, he or she may develop permanent vision loss. Similarly, if a child's celiac disease is not treated, the child's growth may be affected and he or she may develop diarrhea, constipation, and behavioral changes. (See table 3 for these and other health consequences that may occur if these resources are not received by families.)

Advocacy groups told us that if there were gaps in the resources that families received from their health care providers in early childhood, advocacy groups and other community organizations sometimes provided the missing material. For example, one advocacy group initiated a support group for families of children with Down syndrome who also have other medical conditions, such as autism. In addition, advocacy groups provide social development opportunities for children with Down syndrome by hosting playgroups, providing information about the Special Olympics to families, and sponsoring members to attend national and state conferences. Some community organizations also offer social opportunities for children, including children with Down syndrome, such as baseball leagues and swimming classes.

Advocacy Groups and National Survey Results Indicate Families May Face Barriers Such as Outdated or Inaccurate Information

According to Down syndrome advocacy groups, families in their communities may face barriers that can prevent them from using available resources, which can have a significant impact on the child and the family. (See table 4.) For example, barriers such as outdated or inaccurate information may lead parents to have a limited understanding of their child's Down syndrome diagnosis and, as a result, underestimate their child's potential. Important resources, such as early intervention therapy services and parent support groups, can be out of reach for some families who face barriers. For instance, advocacy groups identified barriers related to difficulty communicating in English, a lack of transportation, lengthy travel times to appointments (because of distance to resources or geographic location), or busy work schedules (which prevent them from accessing certain resources, such as early intervention therapy services and doctor appointments, that may only be available during the workweek). Furthermore, advocacy groups mentioned that culture can be a barrier to accessing resources. For example, in some communities, parents of children with Down syndrome from other countries were reluctant to seek resources because of concerns about their community's social acceptance of people with Down syndrome.

**Table 4. Barriers Commonly Cited by Advocacy
Groups in Selected Communities**

Barriers	Number of advocacy groups that cited barrier
Outdated or inaccurate information	7 of 12
Lack of insurance or barriers to access to care	7 of 12
Lack of transportation	7 of 12
Lack of adequate financial resources	6 of 12
Difficulty communicating in English	6 of 12
Negative attitudes about Down syndrome	6 of 12
Lack of technology access (e.g., computer, Internet, telephone)	5 of 12
Inability to recognize or connect with resources	5 of 12
Cultural differences	5 of 12
Distance to resources, geographic location	4 of 12
Limited time	4 of 12

Source: GAO analysis of information provided by 12 advocacy groups.
Note: Barriers cited by fewer than 4 of the advocacy groups were not included.

Results of the 2005-2006 NS-CSHCN also showed that families of children with Down syndrome may have trouble accessing needed services. The survey indicated that of the families of children with Down syndrome, birth through age 17, in the United States who needed a referral in the previous 12 months, an estimated 24 percent had problems obtaining referrals. Similarly, of the families whose children needed physical, occupational, or speech therapy in the previous 12 months, 18 percent of their children did not receive all needed therapies. In addition, 16 percent of families of children with Down syndrome reported that they faced barriers using needed resources in the previous 12 months. Some of the most commonly cited barriers were as follows:

- not getting services when their child needed them, not getting needed information,

- having problems finding service providers with needed skills,

- not having the types of services their child needed in their area, and

- having problems in communication between service providers.

Except for problems in communication between service providers, each of these barriers was also mentioned in our interviews with advocacy groups.

Some advocacy groups reported that they and their communities have made efforts to address some of the barriers faced by families related to inaccurate information, financial issues, language, and transportation. To address issues of inaccurate information, one advocacy group initiated an educational outreach program to health care professionals at area hospitals to share important information about Down syndrome, including contact information for local support groups and suggestions for giving a Down syndrome diagnosis to a family. Some advocacy groups made efforts to address financial issues; for example, some advocacy groups arranged for financial advisors to speak to parents at workshops. In addition, some advocacy groups made efforts to address language barriers by translating materials into Spanish and having a staff person available who spoke Spanish.[52] Finally, several advocacy groups told us that they were taking steps to address barriers related to transportation. For example, an advocacy group located in an urban area established four satellite community groups in outlying areas so families could access resources without driving into the city.

AGENCY COMMENTS

We provided a draft of this report to the Secretary of Health and Human Services for comment. In response, the Department of Health and Human Services (HHS) provided us with general comments, which are reprinted in appendix II, and technical comments that we incorporated as appropriate. In its general comments, HHS indicated that our report "presents a thorough summary of the current practices and the successes and challenges faced by children with Down syndrome and their families." HHS emphasized the importance of early intervention services in maximizing children's long-term development. The agency also suggested that cost-benefit analyses, which were beyond the scope of this review, could inform decisions about providing health care services to children with Down syndrome. HHS also suggested that we compare the results of the data analyses from the private health insurance data, the Medicaid data, and the NS-CSHCN data. As we noted earlier in this report, detailed comparisons across the private health insurance and Medicaid data would not be appropriate because of differences in the underlying insurance coverage. Finally, HHS suggested that we provide population sizes for the data sets analyzed, which we have done.

We are sending a copy of this report to the Secretary of Health and Human Services. The report also is available at no charge on the GAO Web site at http://www.gao.gov.

If you or your staffs have any questions regarding this report, please contact me at (202) 512-7114 or bascettac@gao.gov. Contact points for our Offices of Congressional Relations and Public Affairs may be found on the last page of this report. GAO staff who made major contributions to this report are listed in appendix III.

Cynthia A. Bascetta
Director, Health Care

APPENDIX I: MEDICAID DATA

Figures 7 through 10 show that of the children enrolled in Medicaid in 2007, children with Down syndrome from birth through age 4 received more medical care than children without Down syndrome in the seven states in our study.[1] Children with Down syndrome had more outpatient and office-based services than children without Down syndrome in each state we reviewed. (See fig. 7.) In addition, children with Down syndrome generally had more hospitalizations and a longer average length of stay than children without Down syndrome. (See figs. 8 and 9.) Medicaid expenditures were higher for children with Down syndrome than for children without Down syndrome for outpatient, office-based, and inpatient care. (See fig. 10.)

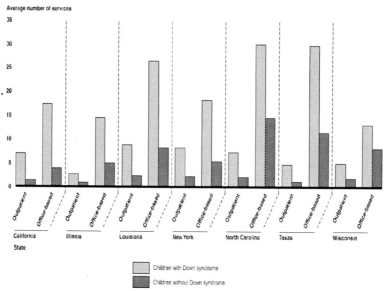

Source: GAO analysis of 2007 Medicaid MAX data.

Figure 7. Average Number of Medicaid Outpatient and Office-Based Services for Children from Birth through Age 4, by State, 2007.

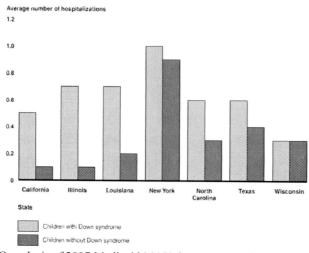

Source: GAO analysis of 2007 Medicaid MAX data.

Figure 8. Average Number of Medicaid Hospitalizations for Children from Birth through Age 4, by State, 2007.

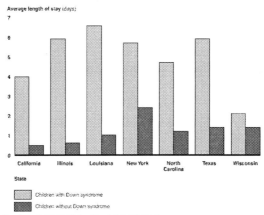

Source: GAO analysis of 2007 Medicaid MAX data.
Note: Expenditures represent the average Medicaid payments for office-based, outpatient, and inpatient care made under fee-for-service arrangements.

Figure 9. Average Length of Medicaid Hospital Stay for Children from Birth through Age 4, by State, 2007.

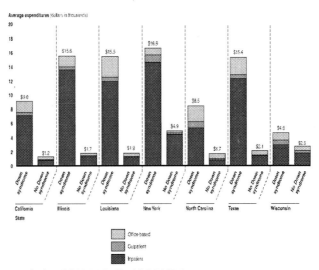

Source: GAO analysis of 2007 Medicaid MAX data.
Note: Expenditures represent the average Medicaid payments for office-based, outpatient, and inpatient care made under fee-for-service arrangements.

Figure 10. Average Medicaid Expenditures for Office-Based, Outpatient, and Inpatient Services for Children from Birth through Age 4, by State, 2007

APPENDIX II: COMMENTS FROM THE DEPARTMENT OF HEALTH AND HUMAN SERVICES

DEPARTMENT OF HEALTH & HUMAN SERVICES   OFFICE OF THE SECRETARY

Assistant Secretary for Legislation
Washington, DC 20201

SEP 2 4 2010

Cynthia A. Bascetta
Director, Health Care
U.S. Government Accountability Office
441 G Street N.W.
Washington, DC 20548

Dear Ms. Bascetta:

Attached are comments on the U.S. Government Accountability Office's (GAO) report entitled: "Children with Down Syndrome: Families Are More Likely to Receive Resources at Time of Diagnosis Than in Early Childhood" (GAO-10-975).

The Department appreciates the opportunity to review this report before its publication.

Sincerely,

Jim R. Esquea
Assistant Secretary for Legislation

Attachment

<u>GENERAL COMMENTS OF THE DEPARTMENT OF HEALTH AND HUMAN SERVICES (HHS) ON THE GOVERNMENT ACCOUNTABILITY OFFICE'S (GAO) DRAFT CORRESPONDENCE ENTITLED, "CHILDREN WITH DOWNS SYNDROME: FAMILIES ARE MORE LIKELY TO RECEIVE RESOURCES AT TIME OF DIAGNOSIS THAN IN EARLY CHILDHOOD"(GAO-10-975)</u>

The Department appreciates the opportunity to review and comment on this draft report. The report presents a thorough summary of the current practices and the successes and challenges faced by children with Down Syndrome and their families. Following are specific comments:

The report and report title suggest that Down Syndrome patients and families receive more treatment and services than those families without children with Down Syndrome. However, the report then proceeds to note these children are not getting all the services that specialists would recommend.

We are concerned that the report's emphasis on the number of services received will drown out the improved impact from early intervention and the long term benefits. We suggest more context be provided from the previous GAO evaluation cited in footnote 31. If possible cost-benefits should also be discussed. Given the concern about increased health care costs, quoting costs without context is not providing a fair review of the impact of the services and what benefits may be gained.

GAO may also want to provide a hypothesis or make a statement regarding the difference in findings between health insurance (private and Medicaid), health services utilization, and expenditure data for children with Down Syndrome and the survey findings from specialists at Down Syndrome Specialty Care Clinics, advocacy groups, and the National Survey of Children with Special Health Care Needs results.

Finally, we suggest that GAO may want to provide the population size for the data analyzed. For example, what are the total numbers for children with Down Syndrome compared to children without Down Syndrome in both the Medicaid study population and the large private health insurance company study population?

End Notes

[1] Centers for Disease Control and Prevention, "Improved National Prevalence Estimates for 18 Selected Major Birth Defects – United States, 1999 to 2001," *Morbidity and Mortality Weekly Report* (Jan. 6, 2006).

[2] J. Ferguson et al., "Resident Physicians' Competencies and Attitudes in Delivering a Postnatal Diagnosis of Down Syndrome," *Obstetrics and Gynecology*, vol. 108, no. 4 (2006).

[3] Pub. L. No. 110-374, § 2, 122 Stat. 4051, 4051 (2008).

[4] It was beyond the scope of our work to evaluate the extent to which the medical care that the children received was appropriate.

[5] Medicaid is a joint federal-state program that finances health care for certain low-income children, families, and individuals who are aged or disabled. The Centers for Medicare & Medicaid Services is responsible for the Medicaid program and related data.

[6] The seven states were California, Illinois, Louisiana, New York, North Carolina, Texas, and Wisconsin.

[7] To identify children with Down syndrome, we examined the diagnosis codes associated with services provided. In the private health insurance population, we identified the following cohorts of children with Down syndrome: children with Down syndrome under 1 year of age (N=318), 1 year of age (N=358), 2 years of age (N=418), 3 years of age (N=463), and 4 years of age (N=477). In the seven states where we analyzed Medicaid data, the population of children with Down syndrome from birth through age 4 ranged from a low of 261 children in one state to a high of 1,020 in another.

[8] In our analysis of the 2007 Medicaid data, the required minimum period of enrollment for children under 1 year of age was the child's age minus 1 month.

[9] Outpatient care includes services received in facilities such as urgent care facilities, ambulatory surgical centers, and hospital emergency rooms. Inpatient care includes services received in residential health care facilities such as hospitals. Office-based care includes services received in facilities such as physician offices, community health clinics, and school-based health clinics. For our analysis, we classified each service based on the type of facility in which it was provided. For example, in our analysis of the private health insurance claims data, we considered therapy services provided in an outpatient hospital setting to be outpatient care, while the same type of therapy services provided in a physician's office was classified as office-based care.

[10] The reference group of children includes all children from birth through age 4 who did not have a Down syndrome diagnosis.

[11] The specialists varied among the Down syndrome clinics we contacted and included health care professionals such as developmental pediatricians, nurse practitioners, and genetic counselors.

[12] For the purposes of our study, we define Down syndrome advocacy groups as local organizations that have been established to help children with Down syndrome and their families.

[13] For Down syndrome clinics identified an equal number of times, we considered the overall geographic diversity within our group of clinics to make our final selection.

[14] For the purposes of our study, health care providers include primary care professionals, such as family practitioners and pediatricians, and other providers at a hospital, such as genetic counselors and social workers, who interact with the family upon a postnatal diagnosis.

[15] Maternal and Child Health Bureau of the Health Resources and Services Administration, National Survey of Children with Special Health Care Needs, 2005-2006. The NS-CSHCN, a large-scale telephone survey sponsored by HRSA and conducted by the Centers for Disease Control and Prevention, defines children with special needs as those who have or are at risk for a chronic physical, developmental, behavioral, or emotional condition and who also require health and related services of a type or amount beyond that required for children generally. The NS-CSHCN provides information on the prevalence of children with special health care needs in the nation and in each state, the demographic characteristics of these children, the types of health and support services they and their families need, and their access to and satisfaction with the care they receive.

[16] We included survey data for families with children through age 17 to ensure a sufficient number of survey respondents.

[17] Based on the sampling error, the NS-CSHCN-reported percentages are within plus or minus 11 points using a 90 percent confidence interval.

[18] According to the Centers for Disease Control and Prevention, chromosomes are small "packages" of genes in the body. They determine how a baby's body forms during gestation and how, as the baby grows in the womb and after birth, the baby's body functions. Typically, a baby is born with 46 chromosomes. Babies born with Down syndrome have an extra copy of all or part of chromosome 21.

[19] Down syndrome is typically associated with a degree of intellectual disability, usually ranging from mild to moderate.

[20] S. Rasmussen et al., "Setting a Public Health Research Agenda for Down Syndrome: Summary of a Meeting Sponsored by the Centers for Disease Control and Prevention and the National Down Syndrome Society," *American Journal of Medical Genetics Part A*, vol. 146A, issue 23 (2008), 2998-3010.

[21] Maternal and Child Health Bureau of the Health Resources and Services Administration, National Survey of Children with Special Health Care Needs, 2005-2006.

[22] B. Skotko et al. for the Down Syndrome Diagnosis Study Group, "Postnatal Diagnosis of Down Syndrome: Synthesis of the Evidence on How Best to Deliver the News," *Pediatrics*, vol. 124, no. 4 (2009).

[23] J. Ferguson et al., "Resident Physicians' Competencies and Attitudes in Delivering a Postnatal Diagnosis of Down Syndrome," *Obstetrics and Gynecology*, vol. 108, no. 4 (2006).

[24] B. Skotko, "Mothers of Children with Down Syndrome Reflect on Their Postnatal Support," *Pediatrics*, vol. 115, no. 1 (2005).

[25] Skotko et al., "Postnatal Diagnosis of Down Syndrome."

[26] In November 2008, representatives from the following five organizations reached consensus that resources provided to parents of children with Down syndrome at the time of diagnosis should be complete, consistent, accurate, and up-to-date: the National Down Syndrome Society (NDSS), the National Down Syndrome Congress (NDSC), the American College of Medical Genetics (ACMG), the National Society of Genetic Counselors (NSGC), and the American College of Obstetricians and Gynecologists (ACOG). Since the consensus conversation, two of the representatives—from NDSS and NDSC—have collaborated with NSGC, ACMG, and ACOG representatives to develop "gold standard" packets of information for health care providers on how to deliver a prenatal and postnatal diagnosis, and a corresponding packet to be given to parents at the time of diagnosis. The prenatal packets were recently published, and the postnatal packet is currently under development.

[27] The exact number of Down syndrome clinics in the United States is difficult to ascertain. However, NDSS lists contact information for 52 Down syndrome clinics for children and adults across the country.

[28] According to a physician at a Down syndrome clinic, it is recommended that children with Down syndrome visit a Down syndrome clinic three to four times in the first year of life, two times in the second year of life, and annually every year after that, if needed.

[29] At the age of 3, children with disabilities transition to special education programs.

[30] 20 U.S.C. § 1433.

[31] GAO, *Individuals with Disabilities Education Act: Education Should Provide Additional Guidance to Help States Smoothly Transition Children to Preschool*, GAO-06-26 (Washington, D.C.: Dec. 14, 2005).

[32] To obtain each of these averages, we calculated the ratios of services for children with Down syndrome compared to children without Down syndrome for each of the 5 years and averaged the ratios.

[33] Outpatient care includes services received in facilities such as urgent care facilities, ambulatory surgical centers, and hospital emergency rooms. Office-based care includes services received in facilities such as physician offices, community health clinics, and school-based health clinics. Some services, such as therapy, can be provided in different types of facilities. For this analysis, we classified each service as outpatient care, office-based care, or inpatient care based on the type of facility in which it was provided.

[34] The age ranges in our analysis are constructed so that, for example, "children under 1 year of age" includes all children from birth up to but not including their first birthday, and so on, with each range consisting of 1 full year.

[35] It is likely that both groups of children received more office-based care than outpatient care because, in general, office-based care includes more routine services, such as office visits and vaccinations, while outpatient care includes less routine services, such as laboratory tests, surgical procedures, and emergency room visits.

[36] Evaluation and management services refer to visits and consultations provided by physicians or other qualified health care professionals. Evaluation and management visits range from straightforward medical evaluations to highly complex patient evaluations and medical decision making.

[37] Children with Down syndrome are more likely to have outpatient surgeries, such as surgeries to insert ear tubes, than children without.

[38] This difference also appears in all other age groups. In addition to this specific thyroid-stimulating hormone blood test, children may have received other types of thyroid tests.

[39] The majority of physical, occupational, and speech therapy services—which accounted for nearly 100 percent of therapy services received—occurred in outpatient and office-based settings. Less than 15 percent occurred in other settings, such as the child's home.

[40] While overall patterns of utilization are consistent between the private health insurance company and Medicaid, more detailed comparisons of the data, such as a more detailed comparison of therapy services, cannot be made because of differences in insurance coverage as well as differences in how services are recorded and accounted for.

[41] Inpatient care includes services received in residential health care facilities, such as hospitals.

[42] To obtain each of these averages, we calculated the ratios of services for children with Down syndrome compared to children without Down syndrome for each of the 5 years and averaged the ratios.

[43] Children with Down syndrome may be hospitalized for longer periods in their first year of life for reasons such as additional screening tests or complex surgeries (such as heart surgery).

[44] We determined the types of hospitalizations based on the diagnosis-related group (DRG) associated with each hospitalization. DRGs are a system for classifying hospital stays based on diagnosis and procedures. Because of a change in DRG coding for 2008, our analysis included DRG data from 2001 through 2007.

[45] The percentage of children hospitalized under this hospitalization type does not represent all the cardiac-related hospitalizations that could have occurred.

[46] While overall patterns of utilization are consistent between the private health insurance company and Medicaid, more detailed comparisons of the data cannot be made because of differences in insurance coverage as well as differences in how services are recorded and accounted for.

[47] Expenditure data were adjusted to 2008 dollars and include the amount paid by the primary insurance company, the deductible, coinsurance, and the amount paid by secondary insurance.

[48] To obtain this average, we calculated the ratios of services for children with Down syndrome compared to children without Down syndrome for each of the 5 years and averaged the ratios.

[49] There are two sets of health care guidelines available to help primary care physicians manage the medical care of children with Down syndrome—the American Academy of Pediatrics guidelines and the Down Syndrome Medical Interest Group guidelines. These serve as a resource for primary care physicians by outlining screenings that should occur and resources that should be shared with families at key points in a child's life. In addition, the guidelines indicate when primary care physicians should refer patients to specialists, if needed.

[50] For the remaining 2 of the 32 recommended resources, half of the 12 advocacy groups reported that the resource was likely to be received, and the other half reported that the resource was less likely to be received.

[51] Hypothyroidism is a condition in which the thyroid gland does not produce enough thyroid hormone.

[52] However, some of these groups noted that they did not have the resources to meet the needs of families who spoke languages other than Spanish.

End Notes for Appendix I

[1] We analyzed fee-for-service claims for services provided in 2007; however, because of coverage variations within and across states, not all services may be covered by fee-for-service plans across all states.

INDEX

Q

R

S

T

U

V